GHOST SIGHTINGS

GHOST SIGHTINGS

Accounts of Paranormal Activity from Around the World

BRIAN INNES

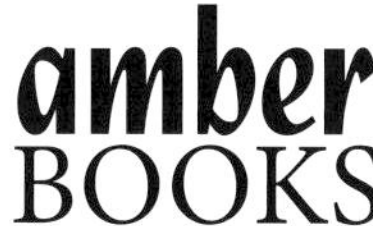

Reprinted in 2019 and 2021

Published by
Amber Books Ltd
United House
North Road
London N7 9DP
United Kingdom
www.amberbooks.co.uk
Instagram: amberbooksltd
Facebook: amberbooks
Twitter: @amberbooks
Pinterest: amberbooksltd

ISBN: 978-1-83886-170-4

Project Editor: Sarah Uttridge
Designer: Sean Keogh
Picture Research: Terry Forshaw

Printed in China

CONTENTS

INTRODUCTION

What is the meaning of the word 'ghost'? The dictionaries seem strangely vague about its origins: they suggest that it is a form of the Germanic *geist* – but that word, in its earliest known use, already had its present meaning as ghost or spirit. Alternatively, it's suggested that 'ghost' is derived from a Nordic word meaning 'angry'. And it is at least arguable that the word comes from the same ancient root as 'gust', signifying a breath of wind – indeed, the Holy Ghost has often been identified by theologians as the 'breath of God'. In this connection, it is interesting how often ghostly phenomena have included a cold breeze, a 'whizzing' in the air, or a sound like sweeping or the fluttering of birds' wings.

Regardless of its derivation, the word is known, and understood, by everybody. What any one person understands by it, however, is another matter. H. H. Price, an Oxford University philosopher who also wrote on parapsychology, pointed out in the 1950s that the question 'Do you believe in ghosts?' cannot be answered until the term is defined – in other words, as C. E. M. Joad, a philosopher contemporary with Price, would have replied: 'It all depends what you mean by ghosts'.

It is undeniable that many thousands of people, sane and reasonably objective, have at one time or another encountered something that 'was not there'. And there are many words besides 'ghost' that can be used to describe this strange something: apparition, wraith, spectre, phantom, spirit, revenant, poltergeist – even hallucination.

GHOSTS OF CULTURES PAST

Ancient peoples firmly believed that many spirits remained at their place of death or burial, as Plato wrote in *Phaedo*: 'You know the stories about souls that roam about tombs and burial grounds.' Not only that, but Plato believed that ghosts were malign spirits: 'It is clearly not the souls of the good, but those of

The *Dialogues* of Pope Gregory the Great contain a collection of ghost stories from early medieval times.

A photograph taken in 1891 of the library at Combermere Abbey. A figure resembling Lord Combermere can be seen sitting in the chair at the same time that his funeral was taking place.

the wicked that are compelled to wander about such places, as the penalty for a bad way of life in the past.'

Christianity complicated the matter by a deliberate misinterpretation of the Greek word *daimonion*. To Socrates in the 5th century BC, the word signified an 'inner voice', a spiritual guide that prevented him from doing wrong, but Christian theorists later identified it as describing a servant of evil, a demon or devil. For centuries, the Church regarded nearly all ghostly manifestations as the operations of evil spirits, or even of Satan himself. People who attracted poltergeist phenomena, or who spoke in trance, were said to be 'possessed', and a great battle had to be fought for their souls. The greatest collection of ghost stories from the early medieval period can be found in the *Dialogues* of Pope Gregory the Great (590–604). Gregory's contemporaries, whose sightings the book describes, frequently declare that they are suffering in Purgatory, but that their suffering has been much relieved by prayers said for their souls. Haunted sites had to be exorcised with bell, book and candle, to drive away the demons that infested them. And when, at last, the Church found itself threatened from within, thousands of innocent people were burnt in the final futile struggle against the imagined demons of Hell.

EVIL INTENT?

In most of the cases described in the following pages, there is no suggestion that an evil spirit is involved. Although many people have fled in fear, these accounts are the work of those who were not frightened, who made an objective report of their observations, and who frequently noted the absence of any sense of empathy between them and the apparition. Even in the most sensational poltergeist cases, researchers have suggested that the 'evil intent' is more likely to have emanated from the human subjects, who were able to draw upon an exterior, impersonal, field of force to evoke the phenomena.

CHAPTER 1

GHOSTS OF CENTURIES PAST

Before the 19th century, people made little attempt to distinguish between kinds of ghost. All were regarded as 'spirits', whether good or evil, noisy or silent, visible or invisible. For this reason, this overview includes phenomena from necromancy to crisis apparitions to poltergeists.

APPARITION AT EN-DOR

Place: En-dor

Time: 800 BC

The oldest written report of the invocation and interrogation of a ghost occurs in the Bible, in the first book of Samuel. Saul, the first king of Israel, had become obsessively jealous of the popularity of his henchman David, and plotted his assassination. Under increasing pressure from the invading Philistines, Saul fell into bouts of melancholia and uncontrollable rage, and David was forced to flee into the wilderness of the Negev, where he gradually attracted a growing band of outlaws.

Looking for guidance, Saul instructed his servants to find him 'a woman that hath a familiar spirit, that I may go to her, and

Gustave Doré's engraving of the apparition of Samuel to King Saul. Saul collapses as the witch summons up the ghost, who demands: 'Why hast thou disquieted me, to bring me up?'

This drawing is believed to be the earliest English representation of the witch of En-dor.

enquire of her'. They knew of a kind of witch in En-dor, so Saul disguised himself in unrecognizable clothing and, taking two bodyguards with him, arrived at the woman's house in darkness. He asked for her help, but she reminded him of his poor treatment of witches and wizards. 'Behold, thou knowest what Saul hath done,' she said, 'how he hath cut off those that have familiar spirits, and the wizards, out of the land. Wherefore then layest thou a snare for my life, to cause me to die?'

Saul swore that no harm should come to her, and begged her to summon up the spirit of Samuel, who had anointed him king. She agreed and summoned up the spirit, but was scared: 'I saw gods ascending out of the earth,' she said, 'and an old man cometh up, and he is covered with a mantle.' Recognizing that this was Samuel, Saul bowed his head. When Samuel asked Saul why he'd disturbed him, Saul answered: 'I am sore distressed; for the Philistines make war against me, and God is departed from me.' Samuel replied: 'The Lord hath rent the kingdom out of thine hand, and given it to thy neighbour, to David, because thou obeyeth not the voice of the Lord... Moreover the Lord will also deliver Israel with thee into the hand of the Philistines; and tomorrow shallt thou and thy sons be with me...'

The Archbishop of Canterbury was visited by the ghost of the long-dead Cardinal Wolsey, three nights after Thomas Wentworth, Lord Stafford, had been beheaded for treason on 12 May 1641.

Hearing this, Saul collapsed and had to be looked after by the witch until his strength returned. Shortly after, the ghost's prophecy came true: three of Saul's sons were killed at the battle of Gilboa, and Saul, mortally wounded, took his own life. The subsequent effective defeat of the Philistines was left to David.

COMMENTARY:

This account leaves us in some doubt as to whether Saul himself actually perceived the ghost, or whether this was a seance at which the witch, in a trance, spoke with Samuel's voice. In any case, it is perhaps an example more of necromancy – the summoning up of a dead spirit for purposes of prophecy, and a practice that was specifically forbidden – rather than a true ghostly appearance: the account makes it clear that the wraith of Samuel did not appear of its own volition, and was not seen subsequently.

THE GHOSTS OF MARATHON

Place: The battlefield at Marathon, Greece

Time: 490 BC and after

Reporter: Pausanius

The battle of Marathon, at which the Athenians under Miltiades defeated the invading Persians, took place in September 490 BC. The Persians lost 6400 men to the Athenians' 192, and the place

For centuries after the battle of Marathon (490 BC), tales were told of how the sounds of fighting echoed around the shrine that had been built for the fallen Greek soldiers.

became a shrine to the fallen Greeks. In about 150 AD, Pausanius wrote a travel guide to Greece. Of the battle site at Marathon, Pausanius wrote: 'In the plain there is a grave for the Athenians, and on it there are slabs with the names of the fallen arranged according to their tribes…

'At this place you can hear all night horses whinnying and men fighting. No one who stays there just to have this experience gets any good out of it, but the ghosts do not get angry with anyone who happens to be there against his will.

'The people of Marathon worship both those who died in the fighting, calling them "heroes", and "Marathon", from whom the county derives its name, but also Herakles, saying that they were the first among the Greeks to acknowledge him as a god.'

The town of Alès in southern France was the scene of one of the earliest psychic investigations of a haunting. After merchant Guy de Torno died, his spirit haunted his home, until the town's prior challenged it.

THE VOICE OF GUY DE TORNO

Place: Alès, France

Time: December 1323

Investigator: John Goby

This 14th-century tale of haunting by an unhappy ghost is particularly interesting in that it involves one of the first recorded cases of psychic investigation, carried out with a degree of scientific caution and recorded with care.

Alès is a town 70km (40 miles) from Avignon in southern France. In December 1323, a merchant named Guy de Torno died there. Within days of his burial, stories began to circulate that his spirit had returned to his home and was haunting his widow.

COMMENTARY:

Battlefields, where so many people have died in both physical and mental agony, and have been buried far from home without due funeral ceremony, have often been notorious places of ghostly hauntings. This account is particularly interesting in that it is one of the earliest reports to suggest that there was a difference between the attitude of the ghosts to visitors who came to the scene to take an inquisitive interest in the phenomenon, and those who were there only by accident.

News of this reached Avignon. The early 14th century was the time of the 'Great Schism', when there were two popes, one based in Avignon and one in Rome. The Avignon pope of the time was John XXII, who, hearing of the occurrences at Alès, appointed John Goby, the prior of the town's Benedictine abbey, to investigate. On Christmas Day, Brother John, accompanied by three of his brethren and followed by a crowd of the citizens of Alès, approached the house of Guy de Torno's widow. His first precaution was to examine the house and garden, to reassure himself that there was no possibility of any trick installations, such as a speaking tube, or of freak sounds being produced by echoes. This done, he appointed several of the more responsible citizens to guard the premises.

The widow had reported that the ghostly voice was most clearly heard in the bedroom. Accordingly, John Goby asked her to lie on the bed, in company with 'a worthy and elderly woman', while he and his three fellow monks sat at each corner. The monks then recited the Office for the Dead, and shortly after heard a 'sweeping' sound in the air – similar, they reported, to that made by a stiff broom. The widow cried out in terror and Goby asked if the sound was caused by the spirit of the dead Guy de Torno. A rather faint voice answered him: 'Yes, I am he.'

While this had been happening, more of the citizens had gathered outside the house, and were asking themselves whether the haunting spirit was in fact a manifestation of the Devil. They then demanded that some of their number be admitted as witnesses of what was taking place. A dozen or so were brought into the bedroom, and stood in a circle around the bed. In reply to their questions, and those of John Goby, the voice assured them that it was not a diabolical entity, but none other than the earthbound spirit of Guy de Torno, condemned to haunt its old home because of the unforgiven sins it had committed there. In particular, it said, it had committed adultery, a sin that, at that time, carried the penalty of excommunication. Unknown to anybody but himself, John Goby had carried Communion bread and wine with him, in a small silver box concealed in his robes – but the ghostly voice told him that it knew he had brought it with him. When Goby indicated that the spirit could be absolved of its sins and receive Communion one last time, it 'sighed, and departed'.

COMMENTARY:

John Goby sent a detailed account of his investigation to the pope in Avignon. The case is unusual for the detachment of Goby's observations, at a time when belief in the corporeal existence of the Devil was particularly strong, and nothing but the complex ritual of exorcism – with 'bell, book and candle' – could normally satisfy both the Church and the people.

From the point of view of the psychical researcher, the haunting was disappointingly brief, allowing no opportunity for further observation of the phenomenon. However, this rather effectively disposes of one of the theories put forward: that Guy de Torno's widow was faking the ghostly visitation – producing the voice by ventriloquism – in order to draw attention to herself. If this had been so, she is unlikely to have given up after John Goby's first visit.

As for the suggestion that the voice had been transmitted by some prankster through a speaking tube, or down the chimney of the house, we must accept Goby's assurance that, considering this a possibility, he had searched the premises thoroughly. Presumably the widow spoke in trance.

An interesting point is that this report speaks, as a considerable number of later ones do, of a 'sweeping' sound in the air.

THE DRUMMER OF TEDWORTH

Place: Tedworth (now North Tidworth), Wiltshire, England

Time: 1662–1663

Victims: John Mompesson, his wife and family

Investigator: Rev. Joseph Glanvill

When John Mompesson, a local magistrate, visited the town of Ludgershall, in Wiltshire, in March 1662, he found a man named William Drury playing a drum in the streets. On questioning him, Mompesson found that the man had a forged permit, and handed him over to the town constable, leaving the drum with the bailiff. Some weeks later, the bailiff sent the drum to Mompesson's house at Tedworth, where his mother encouraged his children to play it.

A section of the frontispiece to Joseph Glanvill's *Saducismus Triumphatus* gives a fantastic portrayal of the Drummer of Tedworth as a devilish being surrounded by lesser spirits.

Returning from a business trip on 4 May, the magistrate was told by his wife 'that they had been much affrighted in the Night by Thieves, and that the House was like to have been broken up'. Three nights later the noise was heard again: 'a very great knocking at his Doors, and the Outsides of his House', which was mostly boarded. Mompesson took his pistols and searched outside, and when he returned 'there was a Thumping and Drumming of the top of his House, which continued a good space, and then by degrees went off into the Air'.

After this, the noise continued on and off for many days, and then was heard in the room where the drum was kept. Mompesson took his bed into the room and watched the drum: 'there it would be four or five nights in seven, and make very great hollow sounds, that the windows would shake and the beds'. Before the drumming began, the family would hear a howling in the air over the house, and then 'the same points of war that is usually beaten when guards break upp, as truely and sweetly, as ever drummer beat in this world,' which lasted for two hours. Soon the noise moved into other rooms, where 'it would imitate the happering of peas upon boards, the shoeing of horses, the Sawyers and many other'.

Mrs Mompesson was expecting a child, and while she was confined to bed the sounds ceased, but in three weeks they returned more violently than ever, shaking the children's beds so that the family thought that they would break up, 'and for an hour together play the tune called "Roundheads and Cuckolds go digg, go digg"... and it will run under the bedsteads and scratch as if it had Iron Talons, and heave upp the Children in the bedd, and follow them from roome to roome, and come to none else but them.'

The phenomena grew even stronger: boards moved, sometimes striking servants or visitors: 'the chaires did walk about, the children's shoes were tost over our heads, and every loose thing thrown about the room.' All the children except the eldest daughter, who was 10 years old, were sent to stay at a neighbour's. Mompesson brought his eldest daughter into his own room, where the spirit hadn't appeared for a month. As soon as Mompesson's daughter was in bed, the ghost was present there, too, and continued for the next three weeks. When the other children returned, 'they were pulled by their night-geer and their haire', and so they had to be sent away again.

The Rev. Joseph Glanvill, chaplain to King Charles II and acquainted with many of the scientists of the day, reported his own observations on the case in his book on witchcraft, *Saducismus Triumphatus* (1681): 'It was as loud a scratching, as one with long Nails could make upon a Bolster. There were two little modest Girls in the Bed, between seven and eleven years old as I guest. I saw their hands out over the Cloaths, and they could not contribute to the noise that was behind their heads.'

Glanvill searched the bed and the wall behind it, but could find nothing: 'After it had scratcht about half an hour or more, it went into the midst of the Bed under the Children, and there seemed to pant like a Dog out of Breath... so strong that it shook the Room and Windows very sensibly.' And then, in the way of such hauntings, the disturbances suddenly ceased, and after April 1663 all was quiet once more.

COMMENTARY:

This case has long been of interest to psychical researchers, because of the detail in which it was recorded, and the objectivity of all those involved. Even John Mompesson claimed that, despite the inconvenience caused by the manifestations, neither he nor his family were ever seriously frightened; and the Rev. Glanvill declared 'that during the whole time of my being in the Room, and in the House, I was under no more affrightment than I am, while I write this Relation.'

In principle, the incident of the Drummer of Tedworth shows all the characteristics of a typical poltergeist manifestation: knockings, or rappings, which gradually increased in intensity, and were followed by scratchings, pulling of hair and bedclothes; the physical movement of furniture and other objects; and the presence of a young – in this case, as in many others, prepubescent – girl, on whom the phenomena seemed to be centred.

There is, however, another, rather more sinister, factor. William Drury, the man whose drum was confiscated, was committed to gaol in Gloucester for stealing pigs, and while there he was visited by a man from Wiltshire, to whom he admitted: 'I have plagued him [John Mompesson] and he shall never be at quiet, till he hath made me satisfaction for taking away my drum.'

Mompesson, in turn, tried to have Drury committed for witchcraft. In a letter dated 8 August 1674, Mompesson wrote: 'When the Drummer was escaped from his Exile, which he was sentenced to at Gloucester for a Felony, I took him up, and procured his commitment to Salisbury Gaol, where I Indicted him as a Felon, for this supposed Witchcraft about my House... on the *Statute Primo Jacobi cap.12*, where you may find that to feed, imploy or reward any evil spirit is Felony...' Unfortunately for Mompesson, the jury acquitted Drury, 'but not without some difficulty'.

Although acquitted of witchcraft, Drury was sentenced to transportation, but somehow – ''tis said by raising storms and affrighting the Seamen' wrote Glanvill – he escaped, and returned to England. Glanvill claims that, on Drury's return, the disturbances began again, but there is no evidence of this. Whether Drury had accomplices who produced the original phenomena while he was in gaol, whether he exerted some kind of psychic influence at a distance, or whether the disturbances were a poltergeist activity, entirely independent of Drury, for which he naturally claimed responsibility, it is impossible at this distance in time to tell.

THE LAST JOURNEY OF MRS VEAL

Place: Canterbury, Kent, England

Time: 8 September 1705

Reporter: Daniel Defoe

In his *True Relation of the Apparition of One Mrs Veal*, as he first reported it in 1706, English writer

Best known for his novel *Robinson Crusoe*, Daniel Defoe was also a journalist and pamphleteer, mostly on political topics. However, one pamphlet, written in 1706, addressed the supernatural.

and journalist Daniel Defoe wrote: 'I am well satisfied as I am of the best grounded Matter of Fact. And why should we dispute Matter of Fact, because we cannot solve things, of which we can have no certain or demonstrative Notions, seems strange to me: Mrs Bargrave's Authority and Sincerity alone, would have been undoubted in any other Case.'

Mrs Bargrave had previously lived in Dover, where she had a close friend in a Mrs Veal; she had moved to Canterbury some months before, and lived in a house of her own. On the morning of 8 September 1705, she was sitting sewing in her favourite chair in the parlour when Mrs Veal, as the clock struck noon, knocked at her door.

Mrs Bargrave was surprised to see her visitor, from whom she had not heard for some time. She went to kiss her, 'which Mrs Veal complyed with, till their Lips almost touched, and then Mrs Veal drew her hand across her own Eyes, and said, "I am not very well," and so waved it.'

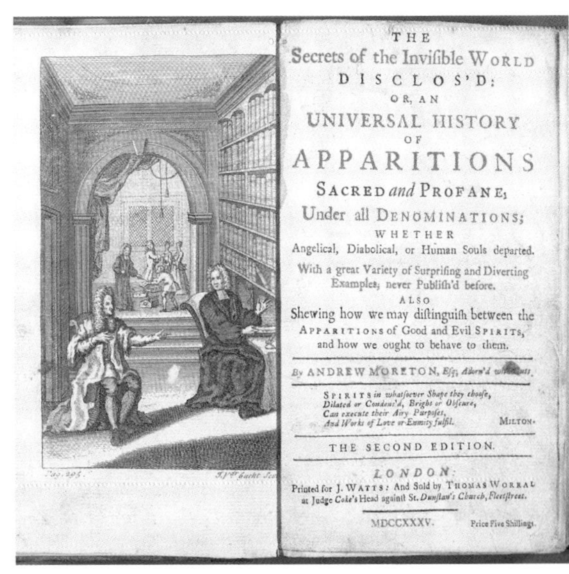

THE
Secrets of the Inviſible WORLD
DISCLOS'D:
OR, AN
UNIVERSAL HISTORY
OF
APPARITIONS
SACRED *and* PROFANE;
Under all DENOMINATIONS;
WHETHER
Angelical, Diabolical, or Human Souls departed.
With a great Variety of Surpriſing and Diverting Examples; never Publiſh'd before.
ALSO
Shewing how we may diſtinguiſh between the APPARITIONS of Good and Evil SPIRITS, and how we ought to behave to them.

By ANDREW MORETON, *Esq*; *Aldern'd* [illegible]

SPIRITS *in whatſoever Shape they chooſe,*
Dilated or Condens'd, Bright or Obſcure,
Can execute their Airy Purpoſes,
And Works of Love or Enmity fulfil. MILTON.

THE SECOND EDITION.

LONDON:
Printed for J. WATTS: And Sold by THOMAS WORRAL at Judge *Coke's* Head againſt St. *Dunſtan's Church*, *Fleetſtreet*.

MDCCXXXV. Price Five Shillings.

Daniel Defoe's experiences of the supernatural were later published, under the pseudonym Andrew Moreton, as *The Secrets of the Invisible World* (1735).

Mrs Veal told Mrs Bargrave that she was about to set out on a journey, and wished to see her friend before she left. Mrs Bargrave was very surprised that Mrs Veal had made the journey on her own, but, said Mrs Veal: 'I had so great a Mind to see you before I took my Journy.'

Mrs Bargrave took Mrs Veal into the parlour, and offered her the chair she had been sitting in. As they talked: 'she would often draw her Hand across her own Eyes' and asked Mrs Bargrave if she thought she looked unwell. But Mrs Bargrave told her, no, she thought that she looked as well as she had ever known.

The two ladies began to talk of their old friendship, and Mrs Veal said that she had come to renew it and to beg Mrs Bargrave's pardon, 'and if you can forgive me you are one of the best of women'.

Mrs Bargrave protested that she had never thought ill of her friend, and readily forgave her; although, she said – somewhat sadly, because she had been brooding upon her misfortunes and loneliness – 'I thought you were like the rest of the world, and prosperity had made you forget yourself and me.' The talk turned to the days when they had been close, the long conversations they had had, and the books they had read together. Among these, Mrs Veal said, she particularly remembered Charles Drelincourt's *Book of Death*, which had given her great comfort, and which she considered the best ever written on the subject.

'As they were admiring Friendship, Mrs Veal said, "Dear Mrs Bargrave, I shall love you for ever"... Then she said she would not take her Leave of her, and walk'd from Mrs Bargrave in her view, till a turning interrupted the sight of her, which was three quarter after One in the Afternoon.'

Defoe reported that Mrs Veal had died, 'of her Fits', at noon on 7 September – that is, exactly 24 hours before the knock came at Mrs Bargrave's front door.

COMMENTARY:

This is an excellent example of a 'crisis apparition'. In the Society for Psychical Research's 1894 *Census of Hallucinations*, many cases of this sort were reported, in which those who had suffered an untimely death subsequently appeared, often with a message of some kind, to close relatives or friends. What is particularly striking is Mrs Veal's awareness of setting out on a journey, and of the importance of settling any differences with her dear friend. No doubt thoughts such as these, inspired by her reading of the *Book of Death*, were much in her mind during her last hours.

THE GHOST OF CAESAR

In Shakespeare's *Julius Caesar*, the ghost of Caesar appears to Brutus in his tent. As defeat later looms in battle, Brutus tells his men: 'The ghost of Caesar hath appear'd to me... I know my hour is come', before falling upon his sword.

'OLD JEFFREY'

Place: Epworth Rectory, Lincolnshire, England

Time: 1716–1717

Victims: Rev. Samuel Wesley and his family

John Wesley, the future founder of Methodism, was a boy of 13, at school in London in December 1716, when his mother wrote of strange happenings at his Lincolnshire home:

'On the First of December, our maid heard, at the door of the dining-room, several dismal groans, like a person in *extremis*, at the point of death... Some nights (two or three) after several of the family heard a strange knocking in divers places, usually three or four knocks at a time, and then stayed a little. This continued every time for a fortnight; sometimes it was in the garret, but most commonly in the nursery...

'We all heard it but your father [the Rev. Samuel Wesley], and I was not willing he should be informed of it, lest he should fancy it was against his own death... But when it began to be so troublesome, both day and night, that none of the family durst be alone, I resolved to tell him of it, being minded he should speak to it. At first he would not believe but somebody did it to alarm us; but the night after, as soon as he was in bed, it knocked loudly, nine times, just by his bedside...

The Old Rectory at Epworth in Lincolnshire. In the winter of 1716–1717 it was the scene of a strange haunting by a noisy presence that John Wesley's sisters nicknamed 'Old Jeffrey'.

The bedroom in Epworth where the knocking of 'Old Jeffrey' was first heard. The haunting included sightings of a man in a nightgown and a creature that resembled a badger.

'One night it made such a noise in the room over our heads, as if several people were walking, then run up and down stairs, and was so outrageous that we thought the children would be frighted, so your father and I rose, and went down in the dark to light a candle. Just as we came to the bottom of the broad stairs, having hold of each other, on my side there seemed as if somebody had emptied a bag of money at my feet; and on his, as if all the bottles under the stairs (which were many) had been dashed to a thousand pieces. We passed through the hall into the kitchen, and got a candle, and went to see the children, whom we found asleep...'

The Wesley family do not seem to have been scared by the presence – not even the younger children, who named it 'old Jeffrey'. The mastiff that the Rev. Wesley brought into the house was less brave: it barked at the sounds when it first heard them, but after two or three days it would tremble and whine, and try to hide behind anyone nearby. Thinking at first that the noise was caused by rats, which had been driven from a neighbour's by his blowing a horn, Mrs Wesley sent for someone to blow a horn like it, but this only caused the knocking to become louder. When the eldest daughter, Molly, heard the rapping at the kitchen door, she opened it cautiously, but saw nothing. When she tried to shut the door, however, she had to force it closed with her knee and shoulder and turn the key, whereupon the knocking began again.

The Rev. Wesley tried questioning the entity, asking if it was his son Sam, but it remained silent. It would, nevertheless, copy any knocks or stamping of feet made by the family.

There were also sightings of strange figures. These were described by daughter Emily: 'My sister Hetty, who sits always to wait on my father going to bed, was still sitting on the lowest step on the garret stairs, the door being shut at her back, when soon after there came down the stairs behind her something like a man, in a loose nightgown trailing after him...'

The notion that something strange might be lurking under the bed was not a new one. Emily also reported her mother seeing an animal 'like a badger, only without any head that was discernible' under her sister's bed. Later it was observed in the kitchen by a servant, but it now looked like a white rabbit.

The manservant, Robert Brown, heard it make sounds 'gobbling like a turkey cock'; two of the daughters described it as being like the winding up of a roasting-jack, while to the Rev. Wesley it was 'like the turning of a windmill when the wind changes'. Finally, towards the end of January 1717, the noises ceased – although a letter from Emily dated 1 April says: 'The spright was with us last night, and heard by many of our family.'

COMMENTARY:

This case is particularly valuable in that it is so fully documented: in a series of more than a dozen letters written by members of the family; in a long entry in the Rev. Wesley's diary; in eight memoranda collected by John Wesley in 1726; and finally in 'An Account of the Disturbances in my Father's House', published by John Wesley in his *Arminian Magazine* in 1784.

As so often in hauntings of this kind, the phenomena seemed to be centred around a teenager, Hetty (Mehetabel) Wesley, then aged 19. She was found to be 'trembling strongly in her sleep', and the sounds often followed her from room to room.

There is a mystery about Hetty's involvement. A letter from daughter Susannah says: 'I should farther satisfy you concerning the disturbances, but it is needless because my sisters Emilia and Hetty write so particularly about it.' The letter from Emily is quoted above, but there is no record of that from Hetty. Was it suppressed by John Wesley, or by Joseph Priestley (the discoverer of oxygen), who published the other letters in his *Original Letters by the Rev.. John Wesley and his Friends…* in 1791, the year of Wesley's death? Priestley wrote that 'Mr John Wesley… was very desirous of getting these letters into his possession… it was taken for granted that he would have suppressed them'. What could the missing letter have revealed about Hetty's attitude towards 'Old Jeffrey' that might have caused distress to the family or to Wesley's followers? We shall never know.

THE DUKE OF BUCKINGHAM

The ghost of the father of George Villiers, Duke of Buckingham, is said to have appeared to one of the king's officers in 1628, warning him of a plot to murder his son. The information was conveyed to Buckingham, but the duke ignored it and was assassinated by a discontented subaltern, John Felton.

'SCRATCHING FANNY'

Place: Cock Lane, London, England

Time: 1759–1762

Victims: Richard Parsons and his family

Ghosts in white sheets? Spirits that rap once for 'yes' and twice for 'no'? People profiting from alleged ghost sightings? The case of 'Scratching Fanny' features elements that have become the cornerstones of many ghost sightings.

In October 1759, No. 20 Cock Lane in the City of London was occupied by Richard Parsons, a clerk at the church of St Sepulchre, his wife, and his two daughters, the elder of whom, Elizabeth, was about 11 years old. A couple who introduced themselves

GAS METER MANUFACTURER
COALS

as Mr and Mrs William Kent took lodgings there, explaining that they had just come to London from Norfolk.

It was not long before William Kent revealed to Parsons that he and 'Mrs Kent' – Fanny – were not actually married. She was the sister of his former wife Elizabeth, who had died in childbirth; Fanny and he had fallen in love, and canon law at that time did not allow a man to marry his deceased wife's sister. However, as proof of their trust in one other, they had made wills in each other's favour.

One day, Kent was out of London to attend a wedding, and Fanny, who was nervous sleeping alone, asked little Elizabeth Parsons to share her bed. Shortly after, they were woken by knocking noises that seemed to come from the bedposts, under the bed and from the wooden panelling around the room. They described the sounds as 'like knuckles rapping', and there were also strange scratching noises. When Fanny complained to Mrs Parsons, she was told that it was probably the cobbler working late next door, but when the sounds continued on Sunday night the family became alarmed.

Fanny was particularly disturbed by the manifestation, and relations between the Kents and the Parsons were troubled by the fact that Richard Parsons was not repaying a loan of 12 guineas that William Kent had made him. There was a row, Kent went to the law, and the Kents moved out. Parsons let his opinion be known that the rappings were caused by the ghost of Fanny's dead sister. When Fanny, who was six months pregnant, fell ill, he declared that it was in punishment for her sin in taking up with Kent.

Parsons' suspicions were strengthened by an experience that he and James Franzen, the landlord of the neighbouring Wheat Sheaf pub, had at the end of January 1760. Franzen had called to see Parsons, but, finding him out, had sat for a while with Mrs Parsons. The strange sounds frightened him, however, and he rose to leave. As he reached the kitchen door, he: 'saw something in white, seemingly in a sheet, which shot by him and up the stairs'. The 'something', he said, gave off a glow sufficient to illuminate the clock on the Charity School across the street.

Shaking, he ran back to the Wheat Sheaf and immediately poured himself a glass of brandy. Scarcely had he raised the glass to his lips than he was joined by an equally terrified Richard Parsons: 'Give me the largest glass of brandy that you have,' the clerk gasped. 'Oh, Franzen! As I was going into my house just now I saw the ghost.'

'So did I!' exclaimed the landlord. 'And have been greatly frightened ever since. Bless me! What can be the meaning of it?'

They very soon had reason to believe the meaning of the apparition, because Fanny Kent was dying. She was attended to by the Rev. Stephen Aldrich of St John's Church, along with a doctor and an apothecary. During the next two days she took nothing but a little liquid medicine, prepared by the apothecary and administered by the doctor. On the evening of 2 February, she died, the doctor certifying that she had expired of 'smallpox of a very virulent nature'. Kent ordered a coffin 'both lined and covered', but as a precaution against prosecution for living falsely as Fanny's husband, he asked the undertaker to put no nameplate on it. Fanny was laid to rest in the vaults of St John's.

The noises in the Parsons' house continued, however, and two new lodgers, Catherine Friend and Joyce Weatherall, later testified that they had left in fear. Parsons called in a local carpenter to take out the panelling in Elizabeth's room, but nothing was found behind it, and it was replaced. Then he asked

A 19th-century engraving of the house that was the scene of 'Scratching Fanny's' manifestations. Although the Parsons were found guilty of conspiracy, there is little evidence of deliberate fraud.

The front room of the Parsons' house. The scratching sounds were heard coming from behind the panelling in the right-hand corner, but nothing could be found when the panelling was stripped away.

for the help of the rector of St Bartholomew the Great, the Rev. John Moore.

Moore claimed to have some knowledge of this kind of phenomena: he was a follower of John Wesley, whose father Samuel had been plagued by similar strange noises at Epworth Rectory 40 years before. With the assistance of Mary Frazer, who was helping to look after Elizabeth Parsons, Moore established a means of communication with the ghost – one that has subsequently been employed by innumerable investigators: asked a question, the entity was to make one rap for 'yes', and two for 'no'.

There now began a series of seances, which soon attracted the attention of the neighbours. Moore held many of them in Elizabeth's room, after the girl had been put to bed. The rappings were heard coming from the floor, the walls and the bed itself. Occasionally there was 'a sound as if a large bird was flying about the room'; at other times there was a noise 'like a cat's claws scratching over a cane chair' – which earned the phenomenon the name of 'Scratching Fanny'. By dint of his questions, Moore established that the rappings were caused by

Fanny's spirit, and that Kent had poisoned her with 'red arsenic' in a mug of purl – a concoction of herbs in ale.

It was nearly a year before rumours of his involvement reached William Kent by means of some sensational articles in the *Public Ledger*, a popular news sheet, and he immediately called on the Rev. Moore. Moore assured him that 'there were very strange noises of knockings and scratchings every night, and that there was something behind darker than all the rest'. Kent therefore attended one of the seances himself, and heard the rappings personally accuse him. When he asked if he was likely to be hanged, he was answered with a single knock. 'Thou art a lying spirit,' he cried. 'Thou art not the ghost of my Fanny; she would never have said such a thing!'

By now, the news of 'Scratching Fanny' had spread and crowds began to flock to Cock Lane. At one time or another, the visitors included the Duke of York, the future Bishop of Salisbury, playwright Oliver Goldsmith and politician Horace Walpole, who wrote: 'Provisions are sent in like forage, and all the taverns and ale houses in the neighbourhood make fortunes.' It must be said, however, that the Parsons do not seem to have profited from their notoriety.

The Rev. Aldrich, who had attended Fanny's deathbed, arranged to have an investigation of Elizabeth at his house on 1 February 1762. Among those present was Dr Samuel Johnson, who later wrote an account of the occasion for *The Gentleman's Magazine*. Elizabeth was put to bed, and told she must keep her hands outside the bedclothes: there was no rapping or scratching. The ghost had agreed to knock on her own coffin in the crypt of St John's if the investigators would assemble there at one in the morning; they trooped off there, and waited a long time – but nothing happened. And so they decided, 'in the opinion of the whole assembly, that the child has some art of making or counterfeiting particular noises, and that there is no agency of any higher cause'.

The authorities were at last moved to take action. After a couple more inconsequential seances, Elizabeth was told that, unless some genuine phenomena were manifested at one final seance, 'she and her father and mother would all be sent to Newgate [Prison]'. Not surprisingly, this frightened the child, and she was caught hiding a small board and a piece of stick inside her dress – although the investigators agreed that the sounds she managed to make with these were quite unlike any noises heard previously.

And so, on 10 July, Mr and Mrs Parsons, Mary Frazer, the Rev. John Moore, and several others were tried before the King's Bench in the Guildhall of the City of London, charged with conspiring 'to take away the life of William Kent by charging him with the murder of Frances Lynes by giving her poison whereof she died'. They were found guilty: Rev. Moore was fined heavily, and Parsons was condemned to the pillory, where he would be chained in public as a form of humiliation.

But it seems that the local people remained convinced of the genuine existence of the ghost, and therefore of Parsons' innocence: instead of pelting him with rotten fruit and dead cats, they threw money at him.

COMMENTARY:

This is another historical case that has provoked much discussion among psychical investigators, once again because of the detail in which it was reported. As in so many cases of this type, the focus seems to have been the young Elizabeth Parsons. During the course of the manifestations, she began to exhibit symptoms that were diagnosed as epilepsy, but she may only have been in a trance.

It is possible, of course, that the whole affair was a

Since the 19th century, there have been many sightings of the ghost of a Grey Lady of Hampton Court Palace. But is this image from 2015 a true sighting of the Grey Lady or a glitch in digital photography?

fraud. In his report in *The Gentleman's Magazine* in 1762, Dr Johnson wrote: 'it is, therefore, the opinion of the whole assembly that the child has some art of counterfeiting a particular noise, and that there is no agency of higher cause.' But the incidents began before the differences over money between Parsons and Kent arose – and the Parsons seem to have been alone among the locals in making no profit from the events, so it is difficult to accuse them of deliberate fraud.

ANOTHER GREY LADY

Place: Hampton Court Palace, near London, Surrey, England

Time: 2015

Reporters: Holly Hampsheir and her cousin Brook McGee, both 12, among many others

A ghost may be hundreds of years old, but it can still make new appearances in the 21st century. In 2015, 12-year-old Holly Hampsheir, who was visiting Hampton Court Palace, took a photograph of her cousin Brook McGee in the King's Apartments. To their surprise, when they later looked at the picture, a tall ghostly figure of a lady with long tresses and wearing a grey dress had appeared in the image.

Was this just the most recent of many ghostly sightings, including that of a lady in grey, at Hampton Court? Both Catherine Howard, Henry VIII's fifth wife, and Sybil Penn, a royal nurse, have traditionally been identified as the Grey Lady ghost of Hampton Court. Sybil had looked after Queen Elizabeth I when she had fallen ill from smallpox at the palace in 1562. Sybil is said to have nursed the queen with such devotion that she caught smallpox herself and died the same year. Catherine Howard was said to have been dragged screaming along the Haunted Gallery back to her rooms when the king learned of her adultery. Henry had Catherine beheaded in 1542, when she was 21.

Since the 19th century, there have been numerous reports of manifestations of the Grey Lady being seen at Hampton Court. Residents have reported hearing a spinning wheel, believed to belong to Sybil. Luke Wiltshire, a member of the palace's security team, has heard inexplicable footsteps around the buildings. Annie Heron, a photo librarian, glimpsed a strange figure at the top of a staircase late one night.

An engraving showing the ghost of Catherine Howard (1521–1542) at Hampton Court. The fifth wife of Henry VIII, she was beheaded on her husband's orders after her adultery was discovered.

A depiction of the ghost of Jane Seymour (1508–37) in the Haunted Gallery at Hampton Court. Henry VIII's third wife, she gave him his male heir, Edward, but died following complications after Edward's birth.

Ian Franklin, a first-aider at the palace, has said: 'When I hear over the radio that a visitor has fainted, I always head straight to the Haunted Gallery, even before I'm told the location of the incident. More often than not, that's where it happens.' The gallery's ghost is said to be that of Catherine Howard.

COMMENTARY:

Did Holly Hampsheir's camera really catch the image of a Grey Lady, possibly Catherine Howard or Sybil Penn? It's certainly a ghostly image, but this might be more to do with the quirks of digital photography than the paranormal. Mick West of Metabunk.org claims that the appearance of the Grey Lady is actually the result of taking a panoramic photograph on a smartphone when someone moves in the image. As the camera pans across the scene, it takes many images and stitches them together into a single, final image. However, if something moves while the photograph is being taken, the image will distort. According to West, the figure of the Grey Lady is none other than Brook McGee in one of the panoramic images that has been distorted.

While this undermines using digital photographs as evidence of ghosts, we should also cast a sceptical eye over the kinds of ghosts people think they see.

The Grey Lady only began appearing in the 19th century, after the chapel in which Sybil Penn had been buried had been knocked down and her tomb disturbed. But there may be another reason why she began appearing at that time and dressed the way she was. Before the 19th century, as Lucy Worsley, Chief Curator at Historic Royal Palaces, pointed out in an article in the *Daily Mail* in March 2015, ghosts were most frequently male and were described as appearing in a white sheet. Why a white sheet? Well, anyone buried in the 16th or 17th century would have been buried tied in a shroud from head to foot. After the 19th century, descriptions of ghost sightings often mention the apparition in grey and black formal wear, in keeping with the clothes of mourning of the Victorian period.

It is also interesting to note that from the 19th century, with the beginning of the Spiritualist movement and the use of mediums, many of whom were women, a higher proportion of female ghosts were reported than before.

Were there simply more female ghosts now? Or is there an element in this that the living are seeing what they wish to see and that the ghosts are more a reflection of the time in which they are observed than the time in which they lived? If the 'Grey Lady' really is the ghost of Sybil Penn or Catherine Howard, wouldn't she appear in Tudor garb or a white sheet, not like a Victorian lady? When something unusual appears in a photograph of a famously haunted place, do we too quickly jump to the conclusion that it's a ghost rather than a glitch?

This is not to discredit all of the paranormal occurrences at Hampton Court. There are still the unexplained footsteps that Luke Wiltshire heard and the strange figure that Annie Heron witnessed. Similarly, in 2015, Linda White uploaded photographs onto social media of what appeared to be a ghostly apparition in a photograph she had taken while on a tour of the former penal colony at Port Arthur in Tasmania, Australia. The image showed a boy from the tour sitting on a bed in a prison cell, while a ghostly child figure appeared hunched over on the other side of the room. There have been many ghost sightings at Port Arthur over the years, but some claimed that the photograph was faked or merely a technical glitch that had spliced together the image of the boy on the tour with a display from elsewhere in the museum.

The ruins of the church at the former penal colony at Port Arthur in Tasmania. The colony, closed in 1877, is now known as one of Australia's most haunted places and the site is open for historical and ghost tours.

CHAPTER 2

GHOSTS OF THE 19TH CENTURY

In the 19th century, investigators of psychical phenomena began to regard the manifestations as being of clearly different types. Accounts of sightings became more carefully documented and were approached more scientifically.

THE CHASE TOMB

Place: Bridgetown, Barbados

Time: 1812–1820

Thomas Chase was a well-known landowner on Barbados, but his bad temper and violent behaviour had made him much disliked. When his young daughter Dorcas died, and her coffin was interred on 6 July 1812 in the modest family vault, rumours began to spread locally that the unhappy young woman had starved herself to death in despair at her father's cruelty.

Only a few weeks later, Thomas Chase himself died – too late, rumour suggested – of remorse. The family tomb, a plain stone building in a small churchyard just outside Bridgetown, was once again opened to receive his coffin, and a horrifying scene met the gaze of the mourners. The three coffins it contained had been flung about the vault, with Dorcas's hurled against the back wall.

The ruins of Ecclesgreig House in Aberdeenshire, Scotland. The house is rumoured to be haunted by Osbert Forsyth-Grant, who led a whaling ship to Canada that sank with all lives lost.

At first, the family supposed that they had been victims of tomb robbers, but nothing appeared to have been taken. Moreover, anybody attempting to enter the tomb would first of all have had to hack away the cement used to seal a heavy marble slab at the entrance to the chamber; the seal was intact, and there were no signs that it had been replaced.

Over the next seven years, the tomb was reopened twice to receive the coffins of other members of the family. Each time, the coffins in the vault were found to have been thrown about – even Thomas Chase's massive casket, which is said to have weighed 110kg (240 pounds) – although the marble slab at the entrance appeared untouched.

After the second of these interments, the story of the inexplicable events had spread so widely about the island that the governor, Lord Combermere, decided to mount an investigation. His men searched the vault, but reported that no one could have got into it other than by the entrance. Before

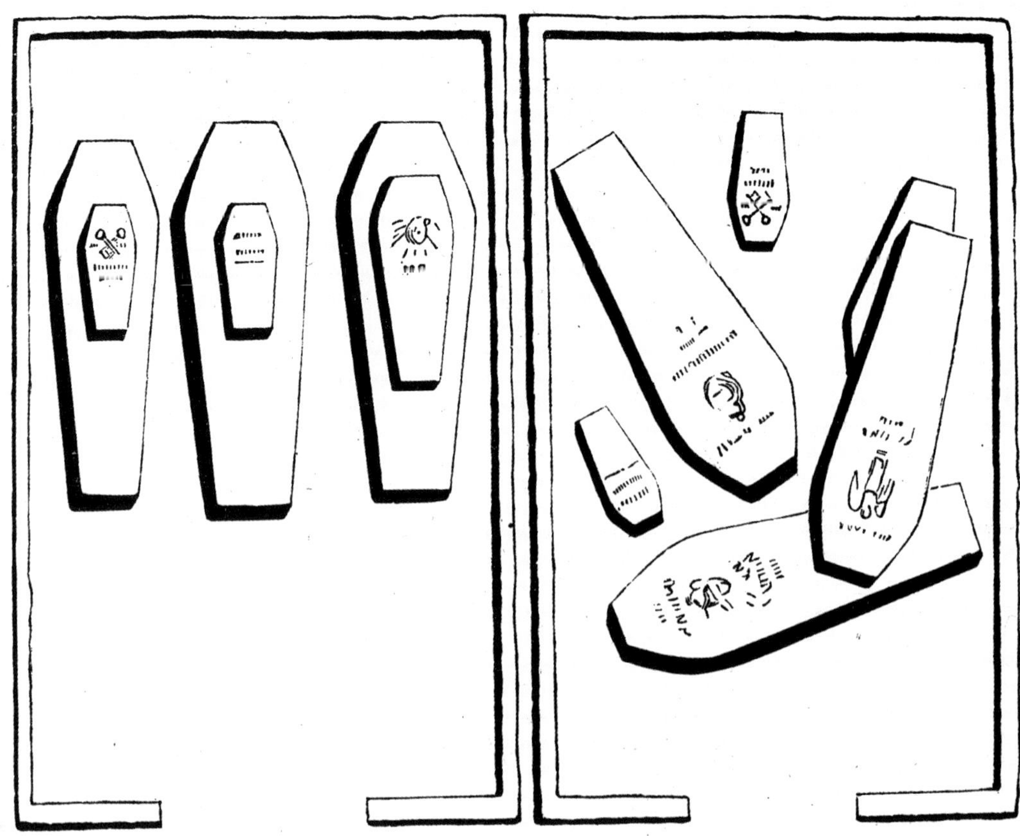

A contemporary drawing of the chaos in the Chase tomb in 1819 showing 'the coffins as they were placed' and 'the coffins as they were found'.

the vault was sealed once more, they sprinkled sand evenly over the floor, to reveal the footprints of any subsequent intruder.

A year later, another member of the Chase family died. This time, when the tomb was opened, the disorder was greater than ever. One of the coffins was completely overturned, some were piled chaotically on top of one another, others leant precariously against the walls. But the sand on the floor was as smooth as ever, without a sign of a single footprint. Lord Combermere, baffled by these events, ordered that all the coffins should be removed from the vault and buried surreptitiously in another cemetery. And ever since that time they have remained apparently undisturbed.

COMMENTARY:

Some writers have cited this series of events as a case of poltergeist activity. Certainly it appears to have centred on the young and unfortunate Dorcas Chase, but no similar incident has been encountered in which the protagonist was dead. It has also been suggested that the disturbances were caused by earthquakes, possibly followed by water entering the vault, but no tremors capable of moving a heavy casket were recorded in those years, and there were never any signs of flooding. Although, apparently, no supernatural phenomena were reported from outside the tomb, this must be classified as a case of haunting, the result of the unhappy circumstances of Dorcas's death, presumably at her own hand.

THE HAUNTING OF WILLINGTON MILL

Place: Willington, Northumberland, England

Time: 1835–1847

Reporter: Joseph Procter

Willington, now within the city of Newcastle-upon-Tyne in the northeast of England, was a separate small town on the River Tyne in the early years of the 19th century. At one time it was famous as the site of a haunted mill: R. T. Stead, in his book *Real Ghost Stories* (1892), devoted no fewer than five pages to a detailed account.

Joseph Procter, the owner of Willington Mill, was a well-known Quaker, far from superstitious, and he kept a diary of the many manifestations that occurred over a period of nearly 12 years. Following the publication of Stead's book, Joseph's son Edmund prepared an edited manuscript of his father's diary, and presented it to the Society for Psychical Research.

The disturbances had begun early in 1835. At this time, the Procters had only one child, a two-year-old boy named after his father; during their occupancy of the mill, Mrs Procter gave birth to three more children – Jane, Henry and Edmund. The nursemaid reported that for some time she had been alarmed by the sound of footsteps in the room above the nursery – a room that was unoccupied, and that subsequently was locked and barred. At first Mrs Procter did not believe her, but, as Mr Procter recorded:

'Before many days had elapsed, however, every member of the family had witnessed precisely what the girl described, and from that time to the present, nearly every day, and sometimes several times in the day, the same has been heard by one of the inmates...'

The steps were so heavy that they caused the nursery window to rattle. Later, other noises were heard: rappings, a weird whistling, chairs moving, and the sound of box lids being closed. Then 'a respectable neighbour' claimed to have seen a transparent white female figure at a second-storey window. Shortly after this, Mrs Procter's mother was lodging at the adjoining house of Thomas Mann, the mill foreman. One evening, Mrs Mann also saw a figure at the same window:

'She called her husband, who saw the same figure passing backwards and forwards and then standing still in the window. It was very luminous and likewise transparent, and had the appearance of a priest in a white surplice. Mr Mann then called out the relative of the family [Mrs Procter's mother] and his own daughter. When they came the head was nearly gone and the brightness somewhat abated, but it was fully 10 minutes before it quite disappeared by fading gradually downwards... It was a dark night, without a moon, and there was not a ray of light... The window blind was close down, and the figure seemed to come through both it and the glass... In walking the figure seemed to enter the wall on either side.'

Soon after this, several occupants of the mill, including young Joseph, felt their beds lifted up in the night, 'as if a man were underneath pushing it up with his back'. They also complained of some unknown presence entering their bedrooms, even though the doors were bolted.

'Jane, about four and a half years old, told her parents that when sleeping with her aunt she one night saw by the washstand at the foot of the bed where the curtains were open, a queer looking head, she thought of an old woman; she saw her hands with two fingers of each hand extended and touching each other; she had something down the sides of her face and passed across the lower part of it.'

Young Joseph then began to hear voices, sometimes very loud, and was afraid to go into his room, even in the daytime. He said that they were phrases such as 'Never mind' and 'Come and get', with little apparent meaning.

On 3 July 1840, when only Mr Procter and a servant were in the house, an acquaintance, Dr Edward Drury of Sunderland, came with a friend, Thomas Hudson, intending to sit all night on the stairs to observe the ghost. Around midnight, they heard the sound of feet knocking on the floor and a rustling as if someone were coming up the stairs.

'I took out my watch to ascertain the time, and found that it wanted 10 minutes to one. In taking my eyes from the watch they became rivetted upon a closet door, which I distinctly saw open, and saw also the figure of a female attired in greyish garments, with the head inclining downwards, and one hand pressed upon the chest, as if in pain, and the other, viz., the right hand, extended towards the floor, with the index finger pointing downwards.

'It advanced with an apparently cautious step across the floor towards me; immediately as it approached my friend, who was slumbering, its right hand was extended towards him; I then rushed at it, giving at the time, as Mr Procter states, a most awful yell; but instead of grasping it, I fell upon my friend, and I recollected nothing distinctly for nearly three

Willington Mill, near Newcastle-upon-Tyne. The Victorians apparently regarded the mill as the most haunted building in the north of England.

hours afterwards. I have since learned that I was carried downstairs in an agony of fear and terror.'

Despite all this, and the fact that there were young children in the house, the Procters endured the disturbances for 12 years, before moving in 1847. On their last night, Mr and Mrs Procter were alone in the house, and heard the sound of boxes being dragged down the stairs, and furniture being dragged about – 'in short, a pantomimic repetition of all the noises incident to a household flitting'.

'A miserable night my father and mother had of it,' wrote Edmund Procter, 'not so much from terror at the unearthly noises, for to these they were habituated, as dread lest this wretched fanfaronade might portend the contemporary flight of the unwelcome visitors to the new abode. Fortunately for the family, this dread was not realized.'

COMMENTARY:

Psychic researcher Harry Price included this haunting in his book *Poltergeist over England* (1945), but it shows only circumstantial resemblances to a typical poltergeist manifestation, and lacks many of the characteristic phenomena, particularly the physical movement of objects. It is also unlike a poltergeist attack in that it lasted nearly 12 years, and there was no child of an age to act as a focus – Joseph was far too young when the events began.

The voices heard by young Joseph may be dismissed by many as childish imaginings. Anticipating this objection, Edmund Procter wrote: 'I can only say that a more truthful boy, or one more transparently honest, I do not think ever breathed.'

Edmund also enquired about subsequent events at the mill, and reported that the mill's foreman, Thomas Mann, had on occasion seen what appeared to be apparitions, but was 'designedly reticent on the subject, and I believe suffered but little...' The house was later divided into two, and eventually knocked down.

This would seem to be a classic case of haunting, but unusual in the detailed record that was kept, and the relative sang-froid of the Procter family. A possible explanation lies in an unfinished sentence in Mr Procter's diary, which he then struck out: 'An infirm old woman, the mother-in-law of R. Oxon, the builder of the premises, lived and died in the house, and after her death the haunting was attributed...'

THE PHANTOM RIDE OF LIEUTENANT B.

Place: Murree Hill Station, Punjab, Pakistan

Time: June–July, 1854

Reporter: General R. Barter

In spring 1854, General Barter, a subaltern, was posted to the hill station of Murree in the Punjab, and occupied a house known as 'Uncle Tom's Cabin' with his young wife. The house had been built two or three years before by a 'Lieutenant B.', who had died in Peshawar at the beginning of the year.

One evening, another officer, Lieutenant Deane, brought his wife to dinner at the Barters' quarters. At about 11p.m., on a clear night with a full moon – 'so bright that you could see to read a newspaper' – Barter accompanied his guests part of the way home. When he took his leave of them, he decided to finish smoking his cigar beside the road, while his two dogs rooted in the undergrowth.

'I had just turned to return home when I heard the ring of a horse's hoof as the shoe struck the stones... and presently I could see a tall hat appear, evidently worn by the rider of the animal. The steps came nearer, and in a few seconds round the corner appeared a man mounted on a pony, with two syces, or grooms. At this time the two dogs came and, crouching at my side, gave low frightened whimpers.'

LORD THOMAS LYTTELTON

Lord Thomas Lyttelton (1744–79) was awoken one night by a sound of fluttering wings. Drawing back the curtains of his bed, he saw the pale ghost of Mrs Amphlett, all three of whose daughters he had seduced. The form approached him and told Lyttelton that he would die in three days' time. At breakfast the following day, he appeared haggard, but on the third day he joked: 'If I live over tonight I shall have jockeyed the ghost...' Shortly before midnight, however, he fell into a fit and died.

THE SINKING OF THE *VICTORIA*

HMS *Victoria*, under the command of Vice-Admiral Sir George Tryon, collided with HMS *Camperdown* during manoeuvres off Tripoli, Lebanon, in 1893. All 358 crew on board and Tryon were killed. There are a number of differing accounts of what ensued in London, several thousands of miles away, that same day. All agree, however, that the figure of Vice Admiral Tryon was seen to walk through his house in Belgrave Square, and was recognized by a number of guests (albeit not by Lady Tryon herself), although he passed by abstractedly, and did not acknowledge them.

The rider was in full evening dress, with a white waistcoat, and wore a tall 'chimneypot' hat. He was mounted on a powerful hill pony, dark brown with a black mane and tail, but was unsteady, and being supported in his saddle by his two servants.

'As they approached I, knowing that they couldn't get to any place other than my own, called out in Hindustani "Koi hai?" (Who is it?). There was no answer, and on they came till right in front of me, when I said in English "Hallo, what the devil do you want here?" Instantly the group came to a halt; the rider, gathering the bridle-reins up with both hands, turned his face, which had hitherto been looking away from me, towards me and looked down on me. The group was still as in a tableau, with the bright moon shining full upon it, and I at once recognized the rider as Lieutenant B…'

The lieutenant's appearance, however, was very different from when Barter had known him, some years before. He was much fatter and, instead of being clean-shaven, he had a dark fringe of beard round his deathly pale face.

Barter sprang forward to climb the bank onto the road, but tumbled and fell in the loose earth. 'Recovering myself instantly, I gained the road… there wasn't a trace of anything; it was impossible for them to go on, the road stopped at a precipice about 20 yards [18 metres] beyond…' He ran back along the road, but there was no trace of anything, nor any sound to be heard. When he returned home, he found that his dogs had run away.

Next morning, Barter called on Deane, who had been in the same regiment as B., and brought the conversation round to the subject of the lieutenant. 'D. replied: "Yes, he became very bloated before his death; you know he led a very fast life, and while on the sick list he allowed the fringe to grow in spite of all we could say to him, and I believe he was buried with it." I then asked where he got the pony I had seen, describing it minutely. "Why," said D., "how do you know anything about all this? You hadn't seen B. for two or three years, and the pony you never saw. He bought him at Peshawar, and killed him one day riding in his reckless fashion down the hill to Trete".'

Barter and his wife remained in 'Uncle Tom's Cabin' for about six weeks, and during that time repeatedly heard the sound of someone riding rapidly down the path. There was never anyone approaching, and they doubted whether anybody except B., who was a reckless rider, had ever attempted it.

'Once when the galloping sound was very distinct, I rushed to the door of the house. There I found my Hindoo bearer… I asked him what he was there for. He said that there came a sound of riding down the hill, which "passed him like a typhoon", and went round the corner of the house, and he was determined to waylay whatever it was. He added: "Shaitan ka ghur hai" (It is a devil's house).'

COMMENTARY:

This is a remarkably detailed and detached account, and it was supported by testimony from Mrs Barter and a Lieutenant Adam Steuart. Although only Barter saw the apparition, Mrs Barter confirmed that she 'several times heard a horse gallop at breakneck speed, during the night, the panting of the horse being quite audible'. Allowing for the possibility that she might have been persuaded by her husband's conviction that the sounds were due to the apparition he had previously experienced, the reaction of the bearer is especially important. So too is the behaviour of the dogs on the first occasion.

As Ernest Bennett says in his book *Apparitions and Haunted Houses* (1939): 'The group and action which General Barter saw was like a scene reproduced or prolonged from the fevered fancies or memories of the man who had now been some months in the grave… The narrative affords a marked example of what has been termed a "local case" – a case, that is, where the appearance of the phantom bears relation rather to the place where it is seen than to the percipients. Nevertheless, the figure in this instance does exhibit cognisance of General Barter's voice and action, as it halts, gathers up the reins, and turns its head to look at the general.'

THE PICTURE OF CAPTAIN TOWNS

Place: Cranbrook, near Sydney, Australia

Time: May 1873

Reporter: Charles Lett

On 5 April 1873, Charles Lett's father-in-law, Captain Towns, died at his home near Sydney. About six weeks later, his daughter, accompanied by a Miss Berthon, went into one of the bedrooms of the house at about 9 p.m. As they entered the room, where the gaslight had been left burning, they saw, apparently reflected on the polished door of the wardrobe, the image of Captain Towns. Charles Lett reports what his wife and her companion saw:

'It was barely half figure – the head, shoulders, and part of the arms only showing – in fact, it was like an ordinary medallion portrait, but lifesize. The face appeared wan and pale, as it did before his death; and he wore a kind of grey flannel jacket, in which he had been accustomed to sleep. Surprised and half alarmed at what they saw, their first idea was that a portrait had been hung in the room, and that what they saw was its reflection – but there was no picture of the kind.'

While the two women stood wondering, Mrs Lett's sister Sibbie came into the room, and before either of the others had time to speak, she exclaimed 'Good gracious! Do you see papa?' One of the housemaids, who was passing the room, was called and asked if she saw anything, and her reply was 'Oh Miss, the master!'

'Graham – Captain Towns's old body servant – was sent for, and he also immediately exclaimed "Oh, Lord save us! Mrs Lett, it's the Captain!" The butler was called, and then Mrs Crane, my wife's nurse, and they both said what they saw. Finally, Mrs Towns was sent for and, seeing the apparition, she advanced towards it with her arm extended as if to touch it, and as she passed her hand over the panel of the wardrobe the figure gradually faded away, and never again appeared, though the room was regularly occupied for a long time after.

'These are the simple facts of the case,' wrote Mr Lett, 'and they admit of no doubt; no kind of intimation was given to any of the witnesses; the same question was put to each one as they came into the room, and the reply was given without hesitation by each. It was by the merest accident that I did not see the apparition. I was in the house at the time, but did not hear when I was called.'

COMMENTARY:

Most remarkable about this report is that no fewer than seven people saw and recognized the apparition, and Mrs Lett was positive that each of the later witnesses saw it independently, without any suggestions from others already in the room. The appearance of the apparition as an apparent reflection is similar to cases in which ghostly figures have been seen in a mirror.

The account does not say whether Captain Towns had suffered pain and distress during his last days – something that would go some way to explain his reappearance. On the other hand, some would say that his spirit had lingered on after his death, and that this was his final leave-taking.

CHAPTER 3

HAUNTED HOUSES

The haunting of houses is a different phenomenon from earlier cases. Rather than brief sightings, the ghosts are usually seen or heard over a long period of time, often centuries, and are a manifestation of someone who suffered intense distress around the time of their death.

A HOUSE IN ATHENS

Place: Athens

Time: 90 AD

Reporter: Pliny the Younger

One of the oldest stories of a haunted house is told by the Roman writer Pliny the Younger in his *Letters*. He wrote of 'a large and spacious house' in Athens where: 'frequently a noise like clanking iron could be heard at dead of night, which if you listened carefully seemed more like the rattling of shackles. At first it seemed to be far off, but it steadily came nearer and nearer, whereupon a ghost appeared in the form of an old man, extremely thin and tattered-looking, with a long beard and bristling hair, rattling the fetters on his feet and hands.'

The courtyard at Glamis Castle, Scotland, where a sealed room is said to conceal a horrible secret. Attempts to discover the room have been firmly discouraged, but ghostly stories abound.

Eventually, the house was abandoned, but, hoping to find a tenant who did not know its reputation, the landlord advertised it to let. A philosopher named Athenodorus arrived from Tarsus. He became suspicious of the low rent being asked and discovered the house's true history; he decided, nevertheless, to take it.

'When darkness fell,' wrote Pliny, 'Athenodorus asked for a couch to be prepared for him in the front part of the house, and after further requesting a lamp, together with his pen and notepad, he advised everyone with him to go to bed…

'The first part of the night passed without incident, then began the clanking of fetters. However, he neither glanced up, nor laid down his pen, completely ignoring the distraction. But the noise grew louder and nearer, until it seemed at the door, and at last in the room where he was. Looking round, he saw the ghost exactly as it had been described to him.

'It stood and beckoned, as if summoning him. Athenodorus signed to it to wait a little, and again bent over his notes and pen, while it stood rattling its chains over his head. He looked round again, and saw it beckoning as before, so without further delay he picked up his lamp and followed it. It slowly stalked along, as if burdened with its chains, and, having turned into the courtyard of the house, suddenly vanished.'

Athenodorus marked the spot where the ghost had disappeared. The next day, he went to the magistrates and advised them to have the place dug up. They found a human skeleton, wound round with chains. The bones were collected together and buried at public expense, 'after which, the ghost having been duly laid, the house was haunted no more'.

COMMENTARY:

This story may well have been old even when Pliny recounted it, and it is fascinating to discover in it all the ingredients of the traditional ghost story of fiction: the philosopher writing late at night by the light of a lamp, the clanking chains, the thin and tattered spectre with long beard and bristling hair... We are reminded of the ghost of Jacob Marley in Charles Dickens's story *A Christmas Carol*.

THE BEAST OF GLAMIS

Place: Glamis Castle, Tayside, Scotland

Time: 17th century onwards

Glamis Castle, where Elizabeth Bowes-Lyon, Queen Elizabeth II's mother, was brought up, is a vast fortified house, the ancestral home of the Earls of Strathmore. The castle has seen more than its share

The end wall of the drawing room at Glamis Castle. The principal painting is of Patrick, third earl of Strathmore, wearing a breastplate, with his sons, one of whom has a deformed arm.

of the turbulent history of Scotland: King Malcolm II was murdered there in 1034; Sir John Lyon was killed in a duel there in 1383; and 150 years later Janet Douglas, Lady Glamis, was burnt as a witch. But legend also tells of a mystery so horrific that it is passed on only to the Strathmore heir on his 21st birthday, and no woman has ever been told the secret.

The castle has its many ghosts. There is the grey-bearded man, whom tradition says was shackled and left to starve in one of the many rooms in 1486. He was seen as recently as the early 20th century, by the wife of the then Archbishop of York. There is the spectre of Janet Douglas herself, known as 'the Grey Lady', who still stalks the long corridors. There is the skeletally thin ghost known as 'Jack the Runner', a black pageboy (presumably dating from the time when young slaves were brought back from the West Indies to be servants in the houses of landowners), and a 'White Lady', who haunts the castle clock tower.

But what is the secret horror of Glamis? Stories of the 'curse of the Strathmores' spread widely during the late 17th century and centred on Patrick, the third earl. He was said to have sat late one Saturday night playing cards with the Earl of Crawford. When a servant came to remind them that it was nearly the Sabbath, Patrick replied that he would continue to play, Sabbath or no Sabbath, and that the Devil himself might take a hand if he pleased. At midnight, with a roll of thunder, the Devil appeared; he told the two earls that they had forfeited their souls, and were condemned to continue gambling in that room until Judgment Day.

As recently as 1957, a servant at the castle, Florence Foster, told a local newspaper that she had heard the earls at dead of night, 'rattling dice, stamping and swearing. Often I lay in bed and shook with fright.'

Patrick is also said to have fathered a deformed child who was kept in a secret chamber until he died at an advanced age. Was this the 'horror'? If so, it seems strange that the secret would have been kept down the centuries, so that the 13th earl, who died aged 80 in 1904, should tell a friend: 'If you could guess the nature of the secret, you would go down on your knees and thank God it were not yours.'

His successor, the 14th earl, is reported to have gone so far as to impart the story to the estate factor, Gavin Ralston, who told the earl's daughter-in-law: 'It is lucky that you do not know and can never know it, for if you did you would not be a happy woman.'

Rumours of a secret chamber abound. A workman came upon a hidden door by chance and, finding that it led to a long passage, explored it – only to emerge shortly after, shaking with terror. When the 13th earl learnt of this, he swore the man to secrecy, and packed him and his family off to the colonies within weeks.

In the 1920s, a party of young people staying at Glamis decided to try to discover the chamber by hanging a piece of linen in each window. When they had finished, they stood outside the castle, but there were still several windows with no linen hanging in them. How were these rooms accessed? When the 14th earl heard what they had done, he flew into a furious rage. Nowadays, visitors to the castle are firmly discouraged from even speaking of the secret chamber, and the mystery of the 'horror of Glamis' remains unsolved.

COMMENTARY:

The story of the deformed child is given flesh by a strange portrait of the third earl that hangs in the castle drawing room. He is seated, wearing a bronze breastplate, and pointing at a distant vista of Glamis. Standing at his left knee is a small, green-clad child. To the right in the picture is an upright young man, but two greyhounds are staring at a figure on the left. This figure also wears a breastplate, but of a curiously malformed shape, and his left arm seems crippled.

Is this the earl's deformed son? Was some genetic defect transmitted down the generations, another, even more hideous, child being born at a later date? Was this child kept hidden from the world in a distant chamber of the castle? And have the Strathmores always feared that the defect would surface again?

THE GREEN LADY OF FYVIE

Place: Fyvie Castle, Aberdeenshire, Scotland

Time: 1601 onwards

Fyvie Castle has been described as the 'crowning glory of Scottish baronial architecture'. The foundations of the castle were laid a thousand years ago, and since the 14th century it has been owned by only five families. The principal architect of the castle as it appears today was Alexander Seton, Lord Fyvie, who became the first Earl of Dunfermline. In 1592 he married Lady Lilias Drummond, the daughter of Lord Patrick Drummond, with whom he lived happily for nine years, and who bore him five daughters.

There was, however, a tradition associated with Thomas the Rhymer, who, in the 13th century, had spent much of his life travelling from one great Scottish house to another, making doom-laden prophecies. In this particular case, Thomas's pronouncement had been interpreted as meaning

'If anyone had told me before I came here that there were such things as ghosts,' wrote a Canadian army officer at Fyvie Castle, 'I should have looked upon that man as an arrant fool.' He came to think differently.

THE EARL OF STRATHMORE

A curious painting of Patrick, Third Earl of Strathmore (1643–95). He is said to have engaged the Devil in a gambling game on the Sabbath, and to have been condemned, with his companion the Earl of Crawford, to haunt the room until Judgment Day.

that no male heir would ever be born within the castle walls – something that is said to have been true for the past six centuries. Impatient that he had no son after nine years of marriage, Alexander Seton began an affair with Lady Grizel Leslie. Learning of the affair, local legend says, Dame Lilias died of a broken heart on 8 May 1601, at the age of 29.

Within six months, Seton had married Lady Grizel. At that time, work was still going on in the building of what is now called Seton Tower, and on the night of 27 October the newly married couple retired to bed in temporary quarters at the top of a spiral stair in the older part of the castle. During the night they both heard the sound of heavy sighs from outside their room and, although Seton called a servant to investigate, no one was found. In the morning, however, Seton and his new wife were dismayed to discover, carved upside down on the stone windowsill in letters eight cm (three inches) high, the name D LILIAS DRUMMOND.

The carving is still there today. The window is more than 15 metres (50 feet) from the ground, and the inscription would have taken a skilled mason several hours to complete, even if he had been able to work from outside without waking Seton and his new wife. No reasonable explanation has ever been advanced for its presence.

From that time onwards, there have been reports of a luminescent Green Lady, who moves up and down the great staircase of the castle. She has been identified, naturally enough, with Dame Lilias – although a portrait, reputed to be of the ghost and dated 1676, bears only a superficial resemblance to that of Seton's first wife. The figure is dressed in a shimmering blue-green gown, and seems to glow with a faint iridescence.

The Gordon family took over Fyvie in 1733, and the phantom was seen more frequently after that – so much so that they adopted her as a family ghost. Colonel Cosmo Gordon, the Laird of Fyvie from 1847 to 1879, told of a lady visitor's maid called Thompson, who reported one morning that she had seen a woman she did not know, in a long green dress, going up the staircase.

'It must have been the Green Lady,' said Colonel Gordon, 'but she only appears to a Gordon.' 'Oh,' replied his visitor, 'I always call my maids "Thompson" as a matter of course. Her real name is Gordon.'

The tradition grew that the phantom was a harbinger of death in the family. One night, Cosmo Gordon saw a shadowy figure beckoning to him in a darkened room, and a few days later his younger brother met the Green Lady walking towards him; as she reached him, she curtsied. Next morning, Cosmo died.

During World War I, a Canadian army officer wrote an account of his experiences while staying at Fyvie. 'If anyone had told me before I came here that there were such things as ghosts, or anything supernatural,' he said, 'I should have looked upon that man as an arrant fool.'

During the first night of his stay, he awoke to find, as he thought, the light on in his bedroom, and rose to switch it off:

'But so doing, I found to my amazement that I had switched it on. I extinguished it once more, but the light remained. The room was illuminated from some other cause and, as I watched, the light got gradually brighter. It was like little flames playing around the pictures, and I could see the colours of the pictures quite distinctly.'

Mr A. J. Forbes-Leith, created Baron Leith in 1905, became the owner of the castle in 1884 and saw the same phenomenon on a number of occasions. He attempted to have it investigated scientifically, but without success. Since his death in 1925, the Green Lady has been seen only occasionally. 'Never combat the supernatural,' Lord Leith once told a visitor. 'Meet it without fear, and it will not trouble you.'

COMMENTARY:

Like Glamis, Fyvie is also said to have a secret, locked chamber that no one may enter, but this – although it may conceal some ancient mystery – is not the room in which Dame Lilias's inscription inexplicably appeared. As for the Green Lady, the pain that Lilias suffered on learning of her husband's infidelity, her death of a broken heart, and the second marriage that followed so quickly upon it – these are more than sufficient to account for her continued appearances down the centuries.

'AWD NANCE'

Place: Burton Agnes Hall, Yorkshire, England

Time: 17th century

Burton Agnes Hall was built at the end of the 16th century by Henry Griffith. After his death, the house was inherited by his three daughters, the youngest of whom, Anne, particularly loved it. Unhappily, while still a young woman, she was attacked and fatally injured by thieves on the road. As she lay on her deathbed, she asked her sisters to promise that her head should not be buried with her body, but should rest in the house.

Understandably, her sisters did not keep the promise. But very soon their life was made unbearable, as Burton Agnes Hall echoed to terrifying noises, groans, crashes and slamming doors. The phenomena became so violent that, with the acquiescence of the local clergyman, the coffin was disinterred. Anne's head was found to be severed

Burton Agnes Hall in Yorkshire. The youngest daughter of its builder, Anne Griffith, haunted the house after her unusual wish for her head not to be buried with her body was ignored.

from her body; although the trunk and limbs had not yet decayed, the head was already a skull.

In accordance with Anne's wishes, the skull was taken to the house. It has been there ever since, except for occasions on which attempts have been made to return it to consecrated ground. Then the phenomena began again, and the cause of them came to be known familiarly as 'awd Nance'. Eventually, the skull was bricked up within the walls of the house, so that it could not be removed, and since then the hauntings appear to have ceased – although the figure of a small woman in a fawn-coloured dress has occasionally been reported in later years.

COMMENTARY:

This is not the only case in which a dying person has requested that their skull should be detached from their body and preserved in their home. Not so very long after the death of Anne Griffith, Theophilus Brome, who died in Chilton Cantelo, Somerset, in 1670, made a similar request. The motive would seem to be almost primitive, recalling the ancient (and far from irrational) belief that the personality – the soul – resided in the head.

DUEL TO THE DEATH

Place: Longleat, Wiltshire, England

Time: 1736 onwards

Longleat, the seat of the Marquess of Bath, is today most famous for its safari park, but it also harbours at least two ghosts. One is the benevolent, non-threatening figure of a man, in the long black gown worn by elderly Elizabethan gentlemen, who haunts the Red Library. He is believed to be John Thynne, the builder of the house, who died in 1580. But there is another ghost, with a grim history. In a passage high in the house – or also, it is said, in the Green Lady's Walk – stalks the ghost of a woman in an agony of grief. Even when she is not seen, some visitors have felt such unbearable sensations of pain and terror in the passage that they have been unable to remain there.

The figure is reputedly that of Lady Louisa Carteret, daughter of the Earl of Granville and wife of the second Viscount Weymouth, who died in

1736, and whose portrait hangs in the house. Lord Weymouth is said to have been of somewhat violent temper; the marriage was not a very happy one, and it appears that Lady Louisa took a lover. Her husband, returning to Longleat without warning after an absence of some days, surprised his wife and the young man together. A fight ensued, weapons were drawn, and Lord Weymouth and the lover duelled up and down the passage, with only Lady Louisa as witness. At last Lord Weymouth thrust his rival through, and killed him. This was no less than murder: hastily and secretly, the body was dragged down to the cellars, and buried there.

Longleat is believed to be the home of two ghosts. One is a man in a long gown who is seen in the Red Library. A benevolent figure, he is thought to be John Thynne, the builder of the house, who died in 1580.

Longleat's second ghost is Lady Louisa Carteret, witness of the murder of her lover by her husband. Dressed in a green gown, her grieving spirit is said to be seen walking in one of the house's high passages.

After this, the guilty Lord Weymouth developed an aversion to Longleat. He moved to Horningsham, a nearby village, and only returned to his estate at infrequent intervals. When Lord Weymouth died in 1751, his son (later the first Marquess of Bath) inherited the property, and found it sadly neglected, the once-renowned formal gardens an overgrown wilderness. It was not long after this that the appearance of the ghost of Lady Louisa was first recorded.

COMMENTARY:

This is the family legend, but there is no documentary evidence to support it: the name of the murdered lover is not known, and there is no record of a missing man. However, in the 20th century, a grim discovery was made at Longleat. In the course of installing central heating in the house, the flagstones of the cellars had to be lifted. Under them lay the bones of a young man, wearing jackboots and clothes of the early 18th century.

The haunting is unusual, in that it is neither the ghost of the murdered man, nor his killer, that appears. However, the terror of the young Lady

Louisa, and the guilt that she felt – and that her husband would have caused her to continue to suffer until her early death – were no doubt sufficient to cause her ghost to linger on in the passage where the murder took place.

The music gallery at Lewtrenchard Manor House, Devon. Margaret Gould exhausted herself restoring the house and now is said to haunt it.

THE BARING-GOULD GHOST

Place: Lewtrenchard, Devon, England

Time: 1795 onwards

Reporter: Rev. Sabine Baring-Gould

The area around Dartmoor in England's West Country is notorious for its ghosts, but few have been

Rev. Sabine Baring-Gould wrote an account of the haunting of his family home by his ancestor Margaret Gould. Residents heard a woman's voice saying: 'It is time for her to have her medicine.'

as well documented as that of Mrs Margaret Gould, the 18th-century ancestress of Sabine Baring-Gould, author of the hymn 'Onward Christian Soldiers'. Margaret Gould's son had dissipated much of the estate by his extravagance, but on his death she set about restoring the family fortunes. She finally exhausted herself with her hard work and, although ill, refused to take to her bed. She died sitting up in her chair.

From that time on she haunted the house, as described by the Rev. Baring-Gould in his *Early Reminiscences* (1923). Frequently, footsteps were heard, passing up and down the Long Gallery. Baring-Gould himself described how, when a member of the family was very ill, the night-nurse was woken from her sleep by a loud knocking at the door, and a woman's voice saying: 'It is time for her to have her medicine'. When she opened the door there was no one to be seen, and nobody in the house admitted having made the call.

In 1918, when two of Baring-Gould's grandchildren were staying in the house, both their nurses insisted on leaving, saying that they had seen a phantom figure bending over the sleeping children. On another occasion, a guest entering the drawing room saw an old lady in a satin dress, and a white-haired man, sitting together, apparently in conversation. They have been identified as Mrs Gould and her friend, old Pastor Elford, who often used to talk together in that room.

COMMENTARY:

Mrs Gould loved her house, and devoted her life to saving it. What should be more natural than that her spirit should have lingered on, to watch over it, and ensure that her descendants cared for it as she had?

THE HORROR OF BERKELEY SQUARE

Place: No. 50, Berkeley Square, London, England

Time: 19th century

Situated at one of the most desirable locations in central London, No. 50 Berkeley Square remained strangely unoccupied for long periods during the 19th century. In November 1872 someone wrote to the magazine *Notes & Queries* to ask if the place was haunted. The enquiry provoked a succession of letters that in August 1879 culminated in a reply by W. E. Howlett, who referred to an article in *Mayfair* magazine the previous May:

'The mystery of Berkeley Square still remains a mystery... The house contains at least one room of which the atmosphere is supernaturally fatal to body and mind. A girl saw, heard, or felt such horror in it that she went mad and never recovered sanity enough to tell how or why.

'A gentleman, a disbeliever in ghosts, dared to sleep in it, and was found a corpse in the middle of the floor after frantically ringing for help in vain. Rumour suggests other cases of the same kind, all ending in death, madness, or both, as the result of sleeping, or trying to sleep, in that room.

'The very party-walls of the house, when touched, are found saturated with electric horror. It is uninhabited save by an elderly man and woman who act as caretakers; but even these have no access to the room. This is kept locked, the key being in the hands of a mysterious and seemingly nameless person, who comes to the house every six months, locks up the elderly couple in the basement, and then unlocks the room, and occupies himself in it for hours.'

WARDLEY HALL

Wardley Hall, Manchester. Legend says that the head of Restoration hellraiser Roger Downes was sent to his home after it had been cut off in a drunken brawl, and that the house was subsequently troubled with violent storms when attempts were made to give it proper burial. In 1779, however, his coffin was opened and the head was found to be still attached to the body.

More details of the incidents referred to soon came to light. J. F. Meehan revealed the contents of a letter written to Bishop Thirlwall in January 1871. It described how a family had hired the house for the London season, as their daughters, one of whom was already engaged, were to be 'brought out'. They invited the young lady's fiancé to stay, and asked one of the maids to prepare an unoccupied room for him. The maid was still busy with her preparations at midnight on the day before his arrival, when piercing shrieks aroused the whole household. Upon rushing upstairs and flinging open the door of the room, they found the unfortunate maid lying at the foot of the bed in convulsions, her eyes fixed, with a terrified stare, on the far corner. She was taken to St George's Hospital, where she died in the morning, refusing to speak of what she had seen, because she said it was far too horrible and distressing to recount.

Next day, the fiancé arrived; he was told the whole story, and the family felt that he should not sleep in that room. Dismissing the story as nonsense, he insisted that he would sleep there, but agreed to sit up until after midnight, and to ring if anything unusual occurred. At midnight, the bell rang once, but faintly. Then, after the family had waited in fearful suspense for several minutes, 'a tremendous peal sounded throughout the house'. Hurrying to the bedroom, they found their guest stretched out in exactly the same place as the maid, convulsed as she had been, and with his eyes fixed in horror on the same corner. Fortunately, the fiancé survived his experience, but, like the maid, refused to describe it, insisting that it was too awful. The family left the house at once.

No. 50 Berkeley Square, London (centre). Until recently this was the premises of antiquarian booksellers, but in the 19th century tales abounded of 'a slimy thing' that slithered up and down the stairs.

As for the 'electric horror' of the party walls, a letter appeared in *Notes & Queries* in 1881. The correspondent reported that, in the early summer of 1880, a ball was given next door at No. 49. A lady and her partner were sitting against the wall, when she suddenly moved from her place and looked round. Her partner was about to ask her why, when he felt impelled to do the same. On comparing their impressions, they agreed that they had both felt very cold, and had felt that someone was looking over their shoulders from the wall behind.

There are other stories. A young girl named Adeline, or Adela, was said to have thrown herself out of the window of one of the top rooms in order to escape the attentions of a wicked uncle, her guardian; it was added that sometimes the ghost of the poor girl could still be seen, clinging to the window ledge. Two sailors were reported to have broken into the empty house to shelter for the night: in the morning, one was found impaled on the railings in the street below, having leapt from the top window in terror, while his companion was found, still in the house, white-haired and mad. It was even rumoured that a 'nameless, slimy thing, too horrible to describe,' slipped up and down the stairs, leaving an evil-smelling trail behind it like that of a snail.

In another tale, a man was said to have gone mad in the upper room. He was waiting for a certain message: other messages appeared on the walls of the room, written by an invisible hand, but the right one never came.

In *The Grey Ghost Book* (1912), Jessie Adelaide Middletone wrote: 'I remember, years ago, hearing a weird story connected with the house, in which the ghost of a child, in a Scotch plaid frock, played the chief part. The poor child was supposed to have been either tortured or frightened to death in the nursery there, and its pathetic little wraith, sobbing and wringing its hands, used to appear to inmates until nobody dared to live in the house.'

After the turn of the century, little more was heard of the haunting of No. 50. And then, in 1969, Mrs Mary Balfour, a respected society lady, told a reporter of the only ghost she had ever seen. Early in 1937, she had moved with her maid into a flat in Charles Street, which adjoins Berkeley Square:

'It was about the time of New Year, and I had come in late when my maid summoned me to the

LITTLEDEAN HALL

Littledean Hall, on the edge of the Forest of Dean in Gloucestershire, is believed to be the oldest continually-inhabited house in Britain – Saxon and Celtic remains have been uncovered in the cellars. According to legend, Littledean Hall was no stranger to death, having witnessed several murders throughout its time. So it is now said to have its full share of ghosts, said to number 11 in all. They include the phantom of a boy, a lady in yellow, a white-clad monk and a phantom coach.

kitchen at the back of the flat. We could see into the back windows of a house diagonally opposite, and in one of them stood a man in a silver-coloured coat and breeches of 18th century cut, wearing a periwig and with a pale, drawn face. He was looking out sadly, not moving. I thought perhaps that he had been to some New Year party in fancy dress, and either had a hangover or some personal trouble. I rebuked the girl for staring at him so. It was only afterward that I found the house was No. 50.'

In 1907, in *Haunted Houses*, Charles G. Harper had written: 'The famous "haunted house in Berkeley Square" was long one of those things that no country cousin coming up from the provinces to London, on sightseeing bent, ever willingly missed.' The address is currently the premises of Maggs Bros Ltd, an antiquarian booksellers, but even 40 years after the booksellers had taken the lease on the premises, they still received three or four calls a month from tourists enquiring after the ghost. 'Unfortunately we can tell them nothing,' said a Maggs Bros spokesperson. 'The so-called haunted room is next to the accounts department; none of us has ever seen, or heard, or felt anything out of the ordinary there.'

COMMENTARY:

The interest aroused by J. F. Meehan's account of the Berkeley Square hauntings persuaded him to ask the Rev. C. F. S. Warren to investigate the stories. In *Notes & Queries* of 19 February 1881, Rev. Warren reported that he had been unable to confirm any of the details, although several of his enquiries remained unanswered, and concluded: 'There remains only the general belief, to all appearance unfounded, that the house is haunted, which it seems to me may well be accounted for by its neglected condition when empty, and the habits of the melancholy and solitary hypochondriac… when it was occupied by him.'

This 'melancholy and solitary hypochondriac' was a Mr Myers, who had rented the house in 1859. At that time he was a well-to-do man about town who was engaged to be married, and who spent the next months decorating and furnishing the house in preparation for his bride-to-be. Unhappily, she jilted him on the eve of the wedding, and he became a silent recluse in his new home. 'At night,' wrote one of the correspondents to *Notes & Queries*, 'he would "keep his assignation with his woe" and flit about the house.'

In 1873 Myers was sued by Westminster Council for unpaid taxes, and the tax collector said that 'the house in question is known as the "haunted house", and has occasioned a good deal of speculation among the neighbours'. Myers apparently died in 1878, and an article in the *Pall Mall* magazine some time later described his last years.

'The disappointment is said to have broken his heart and turned his brain. He became morose and solitary, and would never allow a woman to come near him. The miserable man locked himself away in the ill-fated top room of the house, only opening the door for meals to be brought to him occasionally by a manservant. Generally speaking, he slept during the day and, at night, would emerge from his self-imposed exile to wander, candle in hand, around the house that was to have been the scene of his happiness.'

It seems that the deserted state of the house, and its strange occupant who was never seen, probably gave rise to the stories about it that circulated in the 1870s. But was there really a ghost? A nephew of Mr Myers put forward his opinion that there was a ghost, and that it dated from the 18th century, when the house, with its beautiful Adam fireplaces, was built. This would certainly match with the account given by Mrs Balfour, and would also explain the house's eerie reputation.

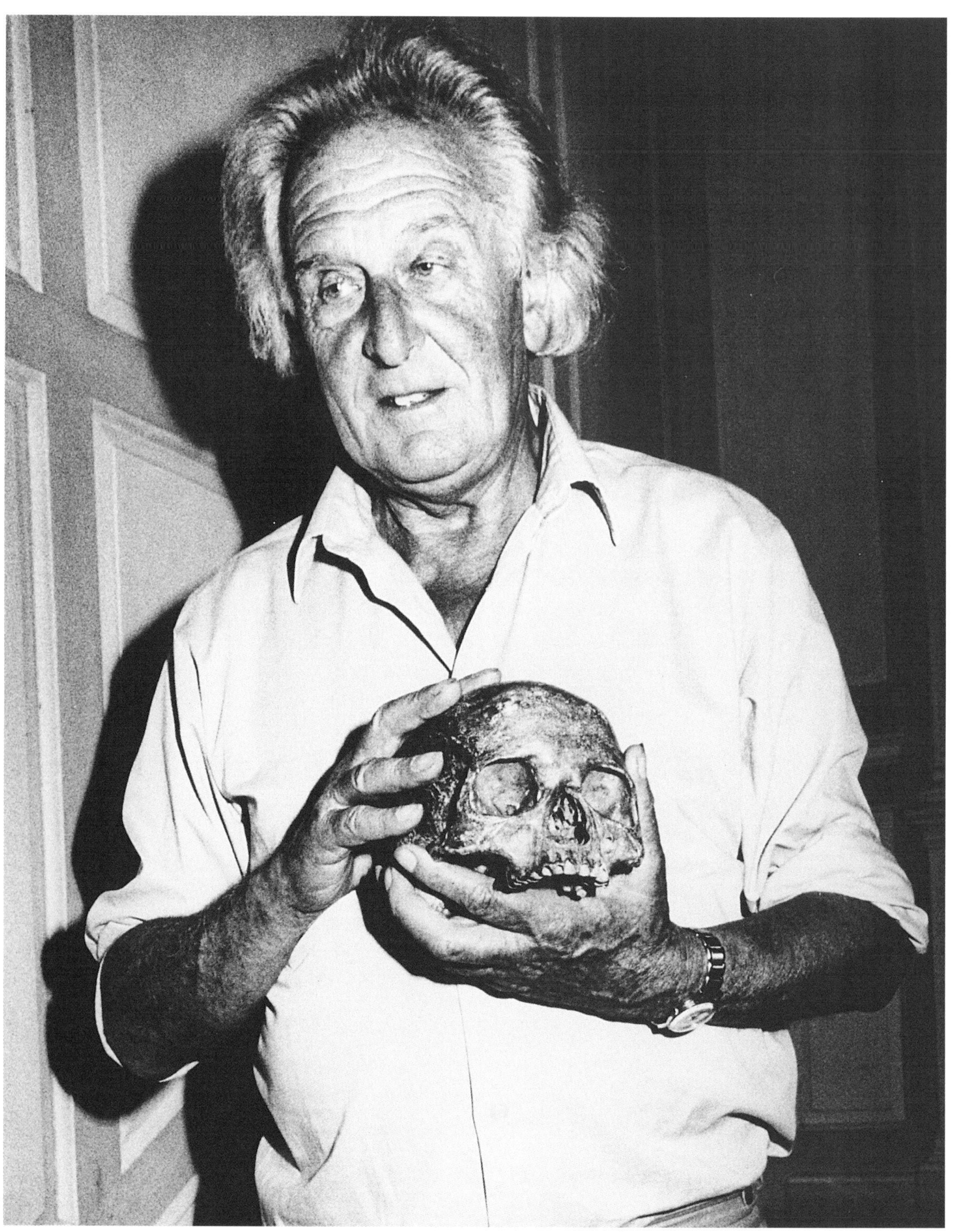

A SCREAMING SKULL

Place: Bettiscombe Manor, Dorset, England

Time: mid-18th century onwards

ABOVE Bettiscombe Manor in Dorset. It is said that death within a year will befall anyone who removes the skull from the house.

LEFT The late Michael Pinney, of Bettiscombe Manor, with the skull. Pinney discovered the skull had probably come from a local prehistoric burial ground.

In 1685, the owner of Bettiscombe Manor, Azariah Pinney, was involved in the Monmouth Rebellion against James II, and as a result was forced into exile in the West Indies. His grandson, John Frederick, returned to the manor early in the 18th century, bringing with him a black slave as a manservant. When the man asked that, on his death, his body should be returned to Africa, Pinney agreed.
It was a promise impossible to keep, however, and when the man died his body was buried in the local churchyard. For weeks after, Pinney and his household were unable to sleep, as bloodcurdling groans and shrieks rang through the house at night. In despair, Pinney had the body disinterred and moved into the manor's attic: this apparently was sufficiently satisfying and the noises ceased.

That is the story as it has come down over nearly three centuries. By 1847, there was only a skull to be shown to a visitor, who was told: 'While this skull is kept, no ghost will invade these premises.' But local legends flourished: it was said that several attempts had been made to remove the skull from the manor, but on every occasion disaster had fallen on the area: storms destroyed crops at harvest time, and cattle and other livestock died mysteriously. It was even claimed that more than one owner of the manor had died within the year. In the 1960s, an old man told how, as a youth, he had heard the skull 'screaming like a trapped rat' in the attic.

Early in the 20th century, the manor was leased to a tenant, who held a wild Christmas party shortly before moving to Australia. During the party, he took the skull – now usually kept in a velvet-lined box in the manor – and threw it into a pond at the side of the house, but in the morning it was found lying on the front doorstep. Some 30 years later, the then owner of the manor, Michael Pinney, and the last descendant of Azariah Pinney to own the house, was visited by three young Australians, one of whom, the son of the former tenant, told him that his father had died suddenly less than a year after moving to Australia.

In 1939, Michael Pinney was disturbed to be asked by a visitor whether the skull had 'sweated blood at the outbreak of war, as it had in 1914?' Nowadays, no one – superstitious or not – is prepared to move the screaming skull from its traditional home.

COMMENTARY:

In the 1950s, at the request of Michael Pinney, the skull was examined by Professor Gilbert Causey of the Royal College of Surgeons. He pronounced it to be that of a young woman, who had died some 3000 to 4000 years before. On a high hill behind Bettiscombe Manor there are remains of prehistoric earthworks. Pinney's theory was that the skull had worked loose from the soil, and been washed down into a stream that flowed through a culvert in an outhouse to the Bettiscombe kitchens.

'The finder may well have tried to get rid of it,' said Pinney, 'only to feel uneasy about the event – perhaps odd things did occur, which convinced him that the skull wished to stay where it had landed. Then the stories began to grow, as news of the skull's arrival spread.'

THE MOST HAUNTED HOUSE IN ENGLAND?

Place: Borley Rectory, Essex, England

Time: 1863 onwards

Investigator: Harry Price

The rectory at Borley, standing across the road from the 12th-century village church, was built by the Rev. Henry D. E. Bull in 1863 to house himself, his wife, and his 14 children. It was a gloomy redbrick edifice with 23 rooms, said to be built on the site of a 13th-century monastery – a claim discredited in 1938 by the Essex Archaeological Society. Local legend told that a monk from the monastery had eloped with a nun from a convent at Bures, 13km eight miles) away; they had been apprehended, the monk beheaded and the nun walled up in the convent, and their ghosts still haunted the area.

Rev. Henry, and his son Harry, who succeeded as rector after his father's death, enjoyed telling the tale of the monk and nun. They may well

Some of the scribblings on the walls of Borley Rectory and Marianne Foyster's attempts to communicate in reply. Commentators have suggested that Mrs Foyster and her daughter were responsible for the writings.

Marianne
light mass
prayers

Marianne
Please help
get

Marianne

I CANNOT UNDERSTAND
TELL ME MORE

Marianne.

I STILL CANNOT UNDERSTAND
PLEASE TELL ME MORE.

have embroidered it, and many of the village schoolchildren grew up convinced of the truth of the story. Two of Harry's sisters related how they had seen a shadowy figure in the rectory garden, moving along what subsequently became known as the 'nun's walk'. In his later years, Harry also told of seeing the nun, together with the phantom coach in which she had eloped, and of having spoken with the apparition of an old family retainer named Amos.

Many years later, former servants and several of the Bull children told of a variety of incidents: strange footsteps in the night, tapping on doors, slaps on the face as they slept. A college friend of Harry Bull stayed at the rectory in 1885 and 1886, and reported (nearly 60 years later): 'stones falling about, my boots found on top of the wardrobe, etc, and I saw the "nun" several times, and often heard the coach go clattering by.'

On 2 October 1928, a year after the Rev. Harry's death, the Rev. G. Eric Smith arrived at Borley with his wife. In a letter to the *Church Times* in 1945, Mrs Smith wrote that neither had thought the house 'haunted' by anything 'but rats and local superstition', but the Rev. Smith was so concerned by the reluctance of his parishioners to visit him that he wrote to the editor of the *Daily Mirror* asking for the address of a psychical expert.

The editor telephoned psychical investigator Harry Price, but he also sent a reporter, V. C. Wall. On 10 June 1929, Wall published the first sensational newspaper story about the rectory. He wrote of 'ghostly figures of headless coachmen and a nun, an old-time coach, drawn by two bay horses, which appears and vanishes mysteriously, and dragging footsteps in empty rooms...'

Borley Rectory in Essex, before being reduced to ruins by fire. The site remains a magnet for ghost-hunters, many of whom are convinced that the phenomena they encounter are genuine.

Investigators Harry Price and Molly Goldney, with the Rev. Lionel A. Foyster, his wife Marianne and their children at Borley in 1931 – the only time Price visited during the Foyster's disturbed five years at the rectory.

Price arrived two days later. Not long after, stones, coins, a glass candlestick and other objects showered down the stairs; all the servants' bells rang in the kitchen, keys flew out of their locks, and rappings were heard on a mirror. He returned to the house several times during the next few weeks, and on each occasion there were similar phenomena, which were duly featured in the *Daily Mirror*.

Within days of the first newspaper report, the Smiths were besieged in the rectory by sightseers arriving from London in coach parties. After enduring the invasion for five weeks, they moved out. The following year, the Rev. Smith left the parish and moved to Norfolk.

The new incumbent at Borley was Lionel A. Foyster, Harry Bull's cousin. With him from Sackville, Nova Scotia, where he had been rector for two years, he brought his 31-year-old wife Marianne, and their adopted daughter Adelaide, aged two and a half. The rectory was in a dilapidated state, and Mrs Foyster took an instant dislike to it. Soon after her arrival the phenomena began again, and now pencilled messages, in a childish scribble, began to appear on the walls. Some were legible – 'Marianne light mass prayers' – but others were impossible to read. Photographs show how Mrs Foyster wrote 'I CANNOT UNDERSTAND, TELL ME MORE' beneath a scrawl that appears to contain the word 'help', only to be answered by a meaningless scribble. Beneath this, without success, Mrs Foyster wrote 'I STILL CANNOT UNDERSTAND, PLEASE TELL ME MORE.'

Rev. Foyster began to keep a diary of events in the house. He recorded crockery disappearing and reappearing, books being moved from one place to another, pictures taken from the wall and laid on the floor, stones and bricks and other objects materialising and striking his wife or himself, and doors found mysteriously locked.

During the five years that the Foysters spent at Borley, around 2000 incidents were recorded, most of them occurring within the first year or two. Harry Price visited the rectory just once during this period, on 15 October 1931, and subsequently wrote to a colleague that: 'although psychologically the case is of great value, psychically speaking there is nothing in it'.

Nevertheless, in 1937, two years after the Foysters had left the house empty, Price rented it and advertised in *The Times* for 'responsible persons of leisure and intelligence, intrepid, critical and unbiased' to form a team of observers willing to spend part of their time there. In his book *Poltergeist over England*, Price wrote:

'I could fill pages with accounts of the thuds, bumpings, "draggings", strange odours, lights... and especially the strange wall-markings that were recorded by my observers. Then there were the phantasms, etc... All were seen.'

All the incidents were sedulously reported in his book *The Most Haunted House in England* (1940). After Price's tenancy expired, the house was bought by Captain William Hart Gregson. He had plans to make it a tourist attraction, with weekly coach parties brought down from London, but on 27 February 1939 the house was destroyed by fire (Gregson himself was accused of arson), leaving only a few smoke-scarred walls standing.

COMMENTARY:

After his death in 1951, the reputation of Harry Price suffered a sharp decline. The council of the Society for Psychical Research asked three of its members to review all the evidence concerning Borley Rectory; their book *The Haunting of Borley Rectory* (1956) was hailed as having shown that the case was 'a house of cards built by the late Harry Price out of little more than a pack of lies'.

Much was made of the fact that the Foysters had previously lived in Amherst, Nova Scotia, the scene of a famous poltergeist manifestation in 1878, and would have been familiar with that story. Indeed, Rev. Foyster used the pseudonym 'Teed' – the name of the owner of the house in Amherst – when writing of the happenings at Borley. Was Mrs Foyster, who disliked the house and also appears to have been unfaithful in her marriage, solely responsible for the poltergeist-like happenings? It was even suggested that the events – and particularly the childish scribblings on the walls – were the work of the three-year-old girl, Adelaide.

The pleasure taken by the Rev. Harry Bull in relating his ghost stories, and the later sensationalism of the *Daily Mirror* reports, only added substance to the claim that the 'haunting' was spurious.
But this was not the end of the story. During the 1960s, a local psychical investigator, Geoffrey Croom-Hollingsworth, became interested in Borley. He and his assistant Roy Potter spent many hours there, over several years, and heard many strange sounds. And then, one clear night, Croom-Hollingsworth saw something.

'In a grey habit and cowl as she moved across the garden and through a hedge. I thought, "Is somebody pulling my leg?" Roy was out in the roadway... and I shouted to him. The figure had disappeared into a modern garage, and I thought that was that, but as Roy joined me we both saw her come out of the other side. She approached to about 12 feet [3.5 metres] from us, and we both saw her face, that of an elderly woman in her sixties, perhaps. We followed her as she seemed to glide over a dry ditch as if it wasn't there, before she disappeared into a pile of building bricks... Roy and I saw the nun quite clearly for a period of about 12 minutes.'

In 1974, Croom-Hollingsworth obtained permission to install tape recorders inside Borley church at night. There is no doubt that the tapes have

recorded a variety of strange sounds, although we have only the testimony of a number of observers that these were not naturally produced. Others have reported similar noises, as well as unexplained photographic images.

As Croom-Hollingworth said: 'I don't give a damn if Price invented things or not. The basic question is – is the place haunted? And you can take it from me it is. I have invented nothing.'

THE LOST ROSE TREE

Place: Ardachie Lodge, Fort Augustus, Scotland

Time: 1953

Investigators: Peter McEwan, Colin Godman

In December 1952, Dr Peter McEwan, a psychologist, and his wife Dorothy, took over an old shooting lodge near Fort Augustus on the shores of Loch Ness in Scotland; they planned to breed pedigree pigs there. They hired a local nanny and a gardener, and by summer 1953 they were sufficiently well established to advertise for a live-in couple, the wife to act as housekeeper and the husband to help with the livestock. The successful applicants were a Mr and Mrs McDonald: Mr McDonald was a postman in London, who gave up his job, and his pension, for the chance of returning to his native Scotland.

The McDonalds arrived at Ardachie Lodge in the evening of 17 August and, after discussing their forthcoming duties, retired early to bed. Soon afterwards, Mrs McDonald heard footsteps in the

'We were told it was haunted, but we didn't put much credence on the story,' said Peter McEwan of Ardachie Lodge on the shores of Loch Ness. But a year after moving in he called the Society for Psychical Research.

The happenings at Ardachie Lodge captured the public imagination and were dramatized for television in 1977 in the series *Leap in the Dark*, starring David Buck.

corridor outside their room; when they came again, she looked out from the door, but saw nothing. She woke up her husband, who also heard the steps, but thought they came from the wall. The couple interrupted the McEwans at a late supper, and asked if there was 'something wrong' with their room. Rejecting all suggestions as to a normal cause for the noises, they were nevertheless persuaded to return to bed.

An hour later, the McDonalds roused the household. They both appeared very frightened, and said that something supernatural had occurred. After going back to bed, they had heard loud rapping on the wall, three or four blows at a time. When the light was switched on, the rappings ceased.

The McEwans decided to move the couple to another room, across the other side of the house, but as soon as she entered the new room Mrs McDonald crossed to the fireplace and pressed her ear to the wall: 'She's in here,' she said. 'There's a woman in this room.' She turned from the wall, and stiffened, staring fixedly into a corner, making beckoning gestures. Then she relaxed, looked around her in a puzzled way, and asked the others if they had seen anything. She said she saw an old woman, with 'straggling grey hair', with 'a cap on her head, a shawl around her shoulders, and… beckoning me to follow her'.

Once again the McEwans suggested moving to another room, but as they gathered at the top of the staircase Mrs McDonald froze with fear again. 'There she is again. Can't you see her? Now she is crawling on her hands and knees with what looks like a candlestick in one hand!' She was so terrified that the others had to force her downstairs into the kitchen, where it was decided they would all spend the rest of the night in Peter McEwan's father's cottage nearby.

On the following two nights, both the McDonalds claimed to hear the rappings again. Dr McEwan was a member of the Society for Psychical Research (SPR) and he contacted their office in London to ask if there were any members who would help him investigate the phenomena. On the evening of 21 August, the household was joined by a Mr Ross and a Mr Mathesen from the SPR. They gathered in the McDonalds' kitchen, where the couple now had their bed.

Soon the whole party heard rappings from the wall. Mrs McDonald became transfixed. As Ross reported in the December 1955 *Journal of the SPR*: 'a lit cigarette dropped from her right hand on to the carpet. Her two arms hung rigid by her side. Her attention was focused, glassily, on the open door.' Suddenly she screamed, and shrank back: she had clearly seen, she said, the figure of the old woman enter the room.

Shortly after, Mrs McDonald retired to bed. As soon as the lights were turned off, leaving only the glow from the kitchen fire, her breathing became laboured, and the rappings began again. After a while she sat up in bed, and asked her husband whether she had been dreaming. She muttered something about 'a rose tree' and 'neglect', and then said 'It's coming to me now – someone has moved a rose tree.'

The McDonalds subsequently maintained that the rappings continued until at least 5a.m., but long before then the investigators had decided to go to bed; they stayed in the guest room where the ghost had first manifested itself to the McDonalds, but reported that they had slept very soundly.

On the following night, the McEwans sat up with the McDonalds once again. Rappings were heard, but it was impossible to detect their source, and a few days later the McDonalds were dismissed and returned to London. The McEwans put the estate up for sale: it was bought by a vet, who carried on farming with success – and apparently no disturbances – and subsequently by a local landowner, who had the house bulldozed to put an end to local gossip.

COMMENTARY:

Dr McEwan made enquiries among his neighbours, and learnt that the previous owner of Ardachie Lodge, an old lady named Mrs Bruen, had often worn a shawl and a small hat, with hair that matched Mrs McDonald's description. Mrs Bruen had suffered from crippling arthritis, and during her last weeks in the house, while having delusions that her servants were robbing her, had crawled painfully along the corridors of the house on her hands and knees, knocking on the floor in search of the supposed missing valuables. She had not, however, died at Ardachie, but had been taken to a nursing home in Inverness.

A neighbour also reported that Mrs Bruen had loved her roses, particularly a rare early-flowering tree that was kept in the greenhouse. Dr McEwan realized that, when he had first arrived at the house, there had indeed been a large old rose tree in the greenhouse that he had asked his gardener to transplant outside, but unfortunately the tree had then died.

Mrs McDonald denied that she had had any previous psychic experiences. How could she have known about the rose tree, and what Mrs Bruen looked like? The only people who could have told her anything in her first few hours at Ardachie were the nanny, Jenny Maclean, and the gardener, Davy Coutts. During the 1970s, Colin Godman investigated the haunting, and made a point of interviewing both.

Jenny Maclean, it transpired, had been in Inverness when the McDonalds arrived, and did not return before they left. And Davy Coutts was at his home in nearby Fort Augustus while the McDonalds were at the Lodge.

This appears to be a genuine case. But what is somewhat unusual is that Mrs Bruen's ghost appeared only to Mrs McDonald, who had no connection with Ardachie Lodge, and who had no previous supernatural experiences of this kind.

SCREAMS IN THE MANSION

Time: 2008

Place: Clifton Hall

Location: Nottingham, England

'The ghosts didn't want us to be there and we could not fight them because we couldn't see them,' said Anwar Rashid about the events in Clifton Hall, the Nottinghamshire mansion he and his family had occupied for only eight months before fleeing.

Mr Rashid, his wife Nabila, their three young daughters and baby son, Mr Rashid's parents and brother had moved into their 17-bedroom, £3.5-million Georgian home in 2007. It was not long before they began to hear the sounds of screams from the mansion's corridors.

'The day we moved in we had our first experience,' said Mr Rashid. 'We sat down in the evening to relax and there was a knock on the wall. We heard this, "Hello, is anyone there?" We ignored it the first time, but two minutes later we heard the man's voice again. I got up to have a look, but the doors were locked and the windows were closed.'

On another occasion, Nabila Rashid went downstairs in the middle of the night to make milk for the baby and thought that she saw her eldest daughter watching television. Nabila called the girl's name, but she did not respond. Nabila went back upstairs only to find her daughter fast asleep in bed. At other times, Mr Rashid and his wife saw ghostly figures in the corridors taking on the shapes of their children. But the final straw came when Mr Rashid and his wife found blood spots on the baby's quilt. 'We didn't even stay that night,' said Mr Rashid. 'We felt that they had come to attack us.'

Mr Rashid called in the Ashfield Paranormal Investigation Network to investigate. Lee Roberts, team leader of the network and a police constable at the time, said: 'Clifton Hall is the only place where I've ever really been scared. It's just got a really eerie feeling about it.' He said that two of his team fainted after independently seeing the same ghost of a boy. Similarly, Darren Brookes of Sovereign Security UK said that staff hired to guard the property reported sightings such as a monk walking through the grounds, a woman in the graveyard falling over, and chairs moving in one of the rooms. 'I've often put officers who know absolutely nothing about the house in there,' said Brookes, 'and after a night on duty they have quit.'

Six months after moving out, Mr Rashid, who was worth £25 million and had made his money through a chain of nursing homes and a hotel in Dubai, had not managed to sell the property and stopped paying the mortgage to the Yorkshire Bank, which reclaimed the mansion.

'When people used to tell me about ghosts, I would never believe them and would say "whatever",' said Mr Rashid. 'But I would have to tell any new owner that it was haunted, having experienced it. I wouldn't be able to sleep knowing that I have kept something so serious from them.'

COMMENTARY:

Knocks on the walls, distant screams in an old building, ghostly figures – all this might seem like classic ghost-sighting material. Perhaps too classic.

The Ashfield Paranormal Investigation Network does not have the reputation of the Society for Psychical Research and Lee Roberts's credibility was undermined in 2010 when he was jailed for 12 months for misconduct for falsifying a signature on a police caution. He is no longer a policeman.

While there had been vague legends about the 18th-century house before, such as ghostly bedtime stories spread while it was used as a girls' boarding school in the 1970s, there were no reports that closely matched those of the Rashid family. Mr Rashid was formerly the director or company secretary of 11 businesses, all of which have been dissolved. Some have suggested that he left his home when his business ventures went bust,

'I've often put officers who know absolutely nothing about the house in there,' said Darren Brookes of Sovereign Security about Clifton Hall, 'and after a night on duty they have quit.'

Nicole Kidman in the 2001 haunted house film *The Others*. When Anwar Rashid reported the spooky events at Clifton Hall, he said: 'The ghosts didn't want us to be there. We were like the family in *The Others*.'

inventing the haunting story to save face about his sudden departure. Mr Rashid, who now lives more modestly in the Nottingham area, has strongly denied this claim. But if Darren Brookes's staff at Sovereign Security are to believed, something really was spooking them at Clifton Hall.

ROOM WITH A BOO

Place: 123 On the Park, New York City, USA

Time: 2014

Observers: Robert Samuel, a former doorman, and other staff and residents

'It's a messed-up place to work because it's haunted,' said one of the doormen at 123 On the Park, an apartment block in the building that for a century was Brooklyn's Caledonian Hospital.

Opened in summer 2014, 123 On the Park was billed as Brooklyn's 'most unique and luxurious address', but it soon gained another reputation. A doorman was watching security-camera footage one night when the motion-sensor lights in a stairwell went on one by one – from the seventh to the ground floor, as if someone were walking down the stairs – but with no one, not even a pet, in sight. A vet living in the building found that her television turned on and off without her touching the remote control and that objects often fell off shelves. One of the building's first residents, who wished to be known by the pseudonym Janine Melnitz, told *The New Yorker* that her bedroom door opened and closed at random, and that she sometimes woke at night to noises in the kitchen. 'Just going down to the employee's locker room gave me an eerie feeling – like a sixth sense,' said Robert Samuel, a former doorman. Other staff and residents commented that certain rooms unnerved them, that they heard footsteps echoing around them and that they felt a presence. As word of this spread, one New York taxi driver dropped off his fare at the block with the words: 'Be careful. It's full of skeletons.'

COMMENTARY:

No paranormal testing has been done at 123 On the Park, so it is not clear if the happenings can be dismissed as technical glitches. But given all the deaths and distressing moments that take place in a hospital, it might not be hard to believe that an apartment block in a former hospital would be a likely haunted location.

However, a more precise, if not wholly serious, motive has been suggested for the hauntings. Perhaps the spirits were 'anti-gentrification ghosts' conjured up by local residents upset that their old hospital, which closed in 2003, had now been replaced by a high-end apartment block.

123 On the Park is situated on the southern edge of Prospect Park in Brooklyn. Before it was turned into an apartment block, it had served Brooklyn for a hundred years as the Caledonian Hospital.

CHAPTER 4

GENTLE GHOSTS

Sometimes ghosts are so unthreatening that the people who experience their presence find it hard to identify them as supernatural phenomena, and may even come to accept them as part of the household.

READING THE BOSTON POST

Place: Boston, Massachusetts, USA

Time: 1830s

Witness: Nathaniel Hawthorne

Nathaniel Hawthorne made his name in 1850 at the age of 46, with the publication of his novel *The Scarlet Letter*. During the 1830s, he had been an official at the Boston Customs House, but had long had ambitions as a writer. Every day, after his official duties, he would call in to the Atheneum Library, a quiet, club-like retreat, where he could read and write for an hour or two.

Another regular was the Rev. Dr Harris, a retired clergyman in his eighties, who sat in the same chair beside the fire each day, reading the *Boston Post*. Although Hawthorne had never spoken to him – conversation being forbidden in the reading room – he had come to regard Dr Harris as almost a permanent fixture, and looked forward to seeing the old gentleman settled calmly in his chair whenever he entered the library.

A photograph capturing the Brown Lady of Raynham Hall, Norfolk, England. The ghost is believed to be that of Dorothy Walpole, sister of Robert Walpole, Britain's first prime minister, who lived nearby.

It came as a great surprise to him, therefore, when one evening, after he had left the library, he was told by a friend that Dr Harris had died some weeks previously. It was an even greater surprise to Hawthorne when, the following evening, he saw the clergyman, as solid and lifelike as ever, sitting in his usual chair with his usual copy of the *Post*.

For weeks Hawthorne continued to encounter the apparition. However, one thing in particular puzzled him. Many of the other regular users of the library, he knew, had been acquainted – some of them quite close friends – with Dr Harris, yet they did not appear to see his ghost. Why, then, had Hawthorne, who was not even an acquaintance, been singled out in this regard? Or did the others also perceive the apparition, but suffer from the same reluctance as Hawthorne to acknowledge it?

Author Nathaniel Hawthorne had become so accustomed to the sight of Dr Harris reading the *Boston Post* beside the fire in the Atheneum Library that he was astonished to learn that the clergyman had died some weeks previously.

Writing about the events later, and looking back on his own behaviour at the time, Hawthorne realized how unwilling he had been to approach the figure, perhaps touch it, even attempt to take the newspaper from its hands. But, he wrote:

'Perhaps I was loth to destroy the illusion, and to rob myself of so good a ghost story, which might have been explained in some very commonplace way.'

After several weeks had passed, Hawthorne became aware that the ghost of Dr Harris appeared to be looking at him, as if it were expecting him to speak or make contact in some way:

'But if so, the ghost had shown the bad judgment common among the spiritual brotherhood, both as regarding the place of interview and the person whom he had selected as recipient of his communications. In the reading room of the Atheneum, conversation is strictly forbidden, and I couldn't have addressed the apparition without drawing the instant notice and indignant frowns of the slumberous old gentlemen around me. And what an absurd figure I would have made, solemnly addressing what must have appeared in the eyes of all the rest of the company an empty chair.'

'Besides,' Hawthorne concluded – somewhat lightheartedly excusing himself on the grounds of social convention – 'I had never been introduced to Dr Harris.'

Hawthorne continued to see the apparition, and to suffer the frustration of being unable to resolve his dilemma, until entering the library one day he found the chair empty, and he never saw the ghost of Dr Harris again.

THE WEEPING WIDOW

An artist's impression of the weeping widow from *The Cheltenham Ghost* by B. Abdy Collins. She was seen by 20 or more people over a period of five years. Several attempts were made to photograph the apparition, but without any success.

COMMENTARY:

This story relies upon the testimony of a single observer, and one who was a writer who wrote many short stories with a supernatural theme. The question arises, therefore: is it true, or a piece of pure fiction? What is striking, for a writer of well-fashioned stories with a satisfactorily dramatic ending, is that the account is down to earth and has no real conclusion. If the story were fiction, surely Hawthorne would have fashioned it in a more 'writerly' way?

So, did Hawthorne truly see the figure of Dr Harris in his usual chair? Some would say that it was a hallucination on his part: accustomed to seeing the old gentleman reading his paper every day, Hawthorne had imagined him still sitting there, long after he had died. But this does not explain how he continued to see him, even after he had been told of his death.

A common explanation would be that the spirit of Dr Harris had somehow become trapped in the place where he had spent so many contented hours, and that he continued to haunt the chair that he had haunted in life. Alternatively, modern psychical theory suggests that the apparition was a sort of 'spiritual recording' impressed by the dead man upon his surroundings, which Hawthorne was able to 'tune in' to, much as one tunes a television set. This also would explain the eventual disappearance of the apparition, as the energy of the recording faded.

THE GHOST DANCE

Place: Nevada, and, later, the Great Plains, USA

Time: 1870–1890, and some years after

A new faith arose among the Paiute Indians of western Nevada in 1870. It began with the dreamer named Ta'vibo, and spread gradually as the Indians became convinced that the western advance of the white man threatened their native culture. Eventually it centred on Ta'vibo's son Wovoka, known to the whites as Jack Wilson, who was regarded as a messiah.

Towards the end of 1888, he became seriously ill. On 1 January 1889, there was an eclipse of the sun, and, as Wovoka later recounted: 'When the sun died, I went up to heaven and saw God and all the people who died a long time ago. God told me to come back and tell my people that they must be good and love one another, and not fight or steal or lie. He gave me this dance to give to my people.'

Wovoka said that the ancestral lands would be returned to the Indians, and there would be a great reunion between the living and their dead relatives and friends. To bring this about, the Indians had only to live according to the precepts Wovoka gave them: give up alcohol, cease farming and the practice of traditional funeral rites – and dance the Ghost Dance.

This, quite unlike any other Indian dance, consisted of a slow, shuffling figure, in which the dancers, both men and women, their fingers linked, formed a series of rings, one within another, and circled to follow the course of the sun. It had to be performed four or five days running, accompanied by chanting, but without any musical instruments. The first Ghost Dance was carried out towards the end of January 1889.

News of Wovoka's message soon spread to many other tribes, eventually reaching the Sioux of the Great Plains. As Dee Brown described in his history of Native Americans, *Bury My Heart at Wounded Knee* (1971): 'In the Drying Grass Moon (9 October 1890)… a Minneconjou from the Cheyenne River agency came to Standing Rock to visit Sitting Bull. His name was Kicking Bear, and he brought news of the Paiute Messiah, Wovoka, who had founded the religion of the Ghost Dance. Kicking Bear and his brother-in-law, Short Bull, had returned from a long journey beyond the Shining Mountains in search of the Messiah…'

Wovoka told them that, the following spring, the earth would be covered with new soil that would bury all the white men. 'The Indians who danced the Ghost Dance would be taken up in the air and suspended there while the wave of new earth was passing, and then they would be set down among the ghosts of their ancestors…'

Kicking Bear introduced something that was not part of Wovoka's original teaching: the 'ghost shirt' of cloth or buckskin, painted with magic symbols, which would protect its wearer against bullets. In addition, the Sioux adopted the deliberate use of hypnotic trance, which was believed to put them into direct communication with the ghosts of their dead. By the end of 1890, the Ghost Dance ceremony was being practised throughout the American West.

The Ghost Dance of the Great Plains Indians in 1893. It was a peaceful rite intended to ensure the return of ancestral ghosts, but it fanned fears of white settlers.

A ghost shirt of the Arapaho people, painted with stars, birds and a turtle. It was believed to protect the wearer against bullets, but was powerless against the shells of the Hotchkiss guns.

COMMENTARY:

The message of Wovoka was essentially a peaceful one, but its spread among the Indians, coupled with the promise of the imminent disappearance of the white man, alarmed officials in charge of the many reservations. At Standing Rock, the local agency representative, James McLaughlin, ordered the arrest of Sitting Bull. In a struggle in the early hours of 15 December 1890, the old chief and 13 of his followers were killed. The rest of his people fled into the Bad Lands to join Kicking Bear. Driven to Wounded Knee Creek by white and Indian troops (the 'metal breasts'), the warriors turned to fight, confident that their ghost shirts would protect them – but they were powerless against the shells of four Hotchkiss guns, and 300 men, women and children were slaughtered.

The Ghost Dance continued for some time among more southern tribes, notably the Kiowa, but the massacre at Wounded Knee had spelt its death knell, and ended the last hope of the Indians.

A SCHOLARLY GHOST

Place: Mannington Hall, Norfolk, England

Time: 10 October 1879

Observer: Dr Augustus Jessop

On 10 October 1879, the antiquary Dr Augustus Jessop was invited to stay at Mannington Hall, an ancient manor house surrounded by a moat that is home to the Earl of Orford. The second Lord Orford, Robert Walpole, had destroyed the tombs of the Hall's previous owners, the Scalmers, in the mid-18th century, and a lady of that family was said to haunt the churchyard looking for her vanished resting place. Until the end of the 19th century, to mollify her, the hearse bearing the coffin of each subsequent earl had to be driven three times around the church before the burial. In an article in the *Atheneum* magazine of January 1880, however, Dr Jessop described a very different ghostly visitation.

The purpose of his visit was to consult some rare books in the library of the Hall. Late in the evening, at his own request, he was left to work alone in a room next to the library, while the rest of the household retired to bed. As he sat making notes, at about 1 a.m., he noticed a hand resting on the table close by his elbow.

Turning his head, Dr Jessop saw: 'a somewhat large man, with his back to the fire, bending slightly over the table and apparently examining the pile of books that I had been at work upon'. The figure was seated close to him, but with its face only partly visible: it had close-cut reddish-brown hair, and wore 'a kind of ecclesiastical habit of thick corded silk, or some such material', with a tight fitting stand-up collar.

Dr Jessop wrote that he realized immediately that the figure was 'not of this world', but felt no fear, only curiosity and keen interest. 'There he sat, and I was fascinated: afraid, not of his staying, but lest he should go.' But, when the antiquary stretched out a hand for one of the books a moment later, the figure, to his great disappointment, vanished.

For five minutes Dr Jessop continued his writing, when suddenly the figure reappeared, in the same chair and attitude as before. There the two sat, ghostly and living scholar side by side, the one still intent upon the books, the other, while writing, trying to think of something to say to his visitor, but somehow afraid to speak. The antiquary finished his last few notes, and dropped the book he was

In the mid-18th century, building work at Mannington Hall manor house in Norfolk destroyed the tombs of the house's previous occupants, the Scalmers. Since then, a woman was said to haunt the churchyard looking for her resting place.

consulting on the table; at this slight sound, the apparition once more vanished. And although Dr Jessop waited some time in hope, it did not return. His research being finished, Jessop carried the pile of books through to the library; then, on second thoughts, he took one back, 'and laid it upon the table where I had been writing when the phantom did me the honour to appear to me'. Then he retired to bed, 'and slept very soundly', although we do not know whether or not the ghost returned to study the book that had been left for him.

COMMENTARY:

This tale incorporates the best elements of ghost reports: there is no suggestion of extraneous phenomena such as wailing, or the clanking of chains – so often attributed to the haunting of ancient houses. The phantom appeared almost unaware of the presence of Dr Jessop, being disturbed by his movement or the noise of a dropped book, but returning as if drawn to the old volumes. Lord Orford, no doubt because of his previous family history, was not a man to encourage tales of hauntings at Mannington Hall, and offered no suggestion to explain the provenance of the ghost – indeed, he later insisted that the figure was that of a manservant named Carlo, who was in search of a nightcap.

This explanation clearly does not stand up, in view of the apparition's silence, its seated presence at the table, and its twice returning.

GHOST TOWN GHOSTS

Place: Silver Cliff, Colorado, USA

Time: 1880 to present day

Investigator: Edward J. Linehan

In 1880, a lode of silver was discovered in the Wet Mountain Valley area of Colorado. Within months a seething township of more than 5000 had sprung up, as prospectors and miners hurried to the area in the hope of making a lucky strike. The town was optimistically named Silver Cliff. The silver soon ran out, however, and the disappointed men left for other, more promising, diggings. Within a generation or so Silver Cliff's population had dwindled to no more than 100, rather less than that of the graveyard on the hill above the town.

Reports of strange happenings in that graveyard, though, date from soon after the first dead were buried there. In the town's first year, a group of miners reported seeing faint blue lights floating above each grave, but their tale was dismissed, on the grounds that they had only just left one of Silver Cliff's many saloons.

But soon other, sober, citizens reported that they, too, had seen the eerie glow over the graves. For many years the tale remained little more than local legend, until an article about the lights appeared in 1956 in the *Wet Mountain Tribune*. The story spread and by 1967 it had reached the *New York Times*. The news of the phenomenon attracted a stream of tourists to the area, many of whom claimed to have seen the ghost lights, and the fortunes of the decayed

Are the faint blue lights hovering over the graves above Silver Cliff, Colorado, a manifestation of the lights of long dead miners still looking for silver? Or are they just a Will o' the Wisp, produced by the spontaneous ignition of methane?

little town began to improve. Two years later Edward J. Linehan, an assistant editor on *National Geographic* magazine, wrote an article describing his own experiences.

On the evening of his arrival, local resident Bill Kleine drove Linehan out to the graveyard. As soon as the car's headlights were switched off, and the two men had climbed out of the car, Kleine exclaimed: 'There! See them? And over there!'

Linehan saw 'dim, round spots of blue-white light'; he stepped towards one, but it vanished, only to reappear gradually. He shone his torch at it, but the beam revealed nothing but an ancient headstone. For the next 15 minutes the two men pursued the elusive glows across the graveyard, but could find nothing to explain them.

Kleine told Linehan that many people dismissed the phenomenon as the reflection of the town lights of Silver Cliff and the nearby Westcliff, but Linehan reported that the lights of the two small towns appeared far too distant to produce the effect. And Kleine insisted that both he and his wife had seen the eerie glow 'when the fog was so thick you couldn't see the towns at all'. Since that time, the shimmering lights have continued to appear to visitors to the graveyard.

COMMENTARY:

A number of theories have been advanced to explain the ghost lights of Silver Cliff. When Westcliff was later furnished with mercury-vapour street lighting, it was suggested that this was somehow reflected in small patches of mist in the graveyard, but at the time that Linehan paid his visit it had not yet been installed, and on one occasion, when a power failure cut off every light in town, the lights still glimmered in the cemetery.

Another theory was that the lights were produced by radioactivity, but a Geiger counter sweep of the whole area proved negative. Some people suggested that the lights were produced by luminous paint, daubed on the gravestones by local hoaxers, but no evidence of this was ever found.

It is possible that the effect is similar to the marsh-lights, or Will o' the Wisp, produced by spontaneous ignition of methane from rotting material. However, the lights do not appear only over new graves, and the bodies of most of those buried in the graveyard have long ago decayed to nothing but bare skeletons.

A very different explanation was put forward by the anthropologist and folklorist Dale Ferguson. He pointed out that the Cheyenne and other native Americans laid their dead to rest on hills they considered 'sacred to the spirits'. Sometimes, indeed, a shaman would know that his own death was near, make his way to the 'dead men's hill', and lie there until his soul was taken from him. And a number of Indian tales, Ferguson said, mentioned 'dancing blue spirits' in such locations.

The old-timers of Silver Cliff, however, have another explanation. The shifting spots of light are the lamps of long-dead miners, still searching desperately for silver.

THE VERSAILLES ADVENTURE

Place: Versailles, France

Time: 10 August 1901

Reporters: Charlotte Anne Moberly and Eleanor Jourdain

Marie-Antoinette, the wife of Louis XVI of France, was guillotined in 1793. Eleanor Jourdain and Charlotte Anne Moberly became convinced that this was the figure they had seen painting at Versailles in 1901.

During August 1901, Charlotte Anne Moberly and Eleanor Jourdain were spending a holiday together in Paris. One fine afternoon, they visited the palace of Versailles, outside the city, which neither had seen. After having toured the palace, they decided to walk across the gardens to the Petit Trianon, a house built in the grounds by King Louis XV, and presented by Louis XVI to his queen, Marie-Antoinette, in 1774.

Deep in conversation, they took a path that led in approximately the right direction. Two men were at work there with a wheelbarrow and a spade; the men directed them straight on, but the ladies were struck by their unusual dress – long, greyish-green coats and small three-cornered hats.

Later, discussing their subsequent experiences, the ladies discovered that at this time they both began to feel somewhat depressed and had an impression of flatness about their surroundings. These feelings were heightened as they approached 'a light garden kiosk, circular and like a bandstand, by which a man was sitting'. Neither liked the look of this man, who wore a cloak and a sombrero-style hat, and they bore right on to another path.

Then Miss Moberly and Miss Jourdain heard the sound of running footsteps behind them. Turning round, they found the path deserted, but noticed someone standing close by: 'distinctly a gentleman… tall, with large dark eyes and crisp, curling black hair'. He also wore a cloak and a sombrero, and smiled in an excited way as he pointed them on towards the Petit Trianon. When the ladies turned to thank him, he had disappeared, although they heard once again the running footsteps. They crossed a bridge over a small ravine, remarking on the small cascade that fell beside it, and finally reached their goal.

The lake in the grounds of the palace of Versailles, dark and brooding just as it was on the day that Charlotte Anne Moberly and Eleanor Jourdain experienced their strange adventure.

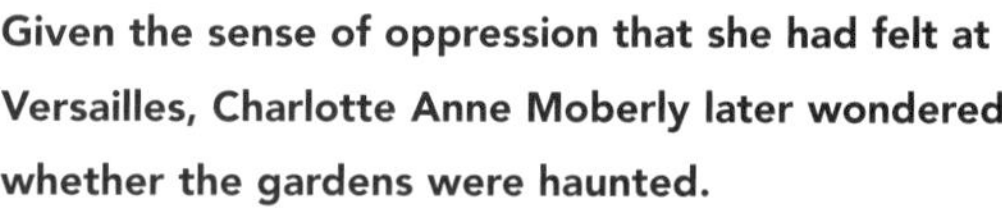

Given the sense of oppression that she had felt at Versailles, Charlotte Anne Moberly later wondered whether the gardens were haunted.

When Eleanor Jourdain revisited Versailles she was surprised to find that the buildings and landscaping were quite different from what she had first seen.

On the terrace, Miss Moberly saw a woman who seemed to be sketching; she looked the ladies full in the face as they passed by. Miss Moberly noticed that, although she wore the dress of a young woman – of light material, with a low-cut fichu neckline – and had a mass of fair hair topped with a white shady hat, she was, though pretty, of somewhat mature years. At this point a young man appeared, who led them to the entrance of the house; there they found themselves swept up on a guided tour with a lively wedding party.

It was only when Miss Moberly sat down, a few days later, to write up her journal, that she recalled the sense of oppression that she had felt, and asked Miss Jourdain: 'Do you think the Petit Trianon is haunted?' The two ladies then discovered that their recollections of 10 August differed in certain details – in particular, Miss Jourdain had not seen the woman sketching. Some months later, discussing the events again, they decided to write independent accounts of their experiences, and compare them.

Miss Jourdain made enquiries in Paris, and was told by a friend that people from Versailles claimed to have seen the phantom of Marie-Antoinette, wearing a pink dress and a large shepherdess's hat, sitting outside the Petit Trianon one August day. On 2 January 1902, Miss Jourdain decided to revisit the scene. Where she and Miss Moberly had noticed the 'light garden kiosk' stood the Temple de l'Amour, which she was sure was not the building she had seen. The ravine, the little bridge and the cascade were no longer there. She turned away from the Petit

Trianon, following the side of a lake until she reached a bridge leading to the Hameau, a miniature country village where Marie-Antoinette and her friends had enjoyed their *fêtes bergères* celebrating rural life by dressing as shepherdesses.

It was as she crossed the bridge that the former sense of eeriness recurred. She noticed two labourers, wearing tunics and hooded capes, loading sticks into a cart; she turned her head a moment to look at the Hameau, and in that instant the men disappeared. She thought she saw a cloaked man moving through the trees, and heard the rustle of silk dresses and the distant sound of a band – but when she enquired a few minutes later, no one knew of any music in the vicinity.

Miss Jourdain returned to Versailles in 1904 with Miss Moberly, and could find none of the features that they had observed in 1901. Even the Petit Trianon differed in its outward appearance. The women were convinced that they had had a supernatural experience.

COMMENTARY:

Both women were well educated: Eleanor Jourdain had read Modern History at Oxford and became principal of her own girls' school in Watford; Charlotte Anne Moberly was principal of St Hugh's Hall (later St Hugh's College) in Oxford.

Another part of the Versailles grounds. Plans for improvements were drawn up in 1774 by the head gardener and closely resemble the scene as remembered by the two women.

They published their independent accounts as *An Adventure*, which has been reprinted several times.

Each edition has attracted comment and criticism. It has been suggested that the ladies did not pay sufficient attention to their surroundings, engrossed as they were in their conversation. One critic has proposed that the men they saw were really the socialite Robert de Montesquiou, who was alive in 1901, and his friends, holding a fancy-dress party in the grounds, much like Marie-Antoinette's *fêtes bergères* – but this hardly explains the presence of the garden labourers.

The date of the experience is important. Miss Jourdain and Miss Moberly visited Versailles on 10 August 1901 – it was on 10 August 1792 that the Paris mob sacked the royal apartments in the Tuileries and imprisoned the royal family.

It is inconceivable that Miss Jourdain, having studied modern history, was unaware of the significance of the date – she may even have remarked upon it to Miss Moberly. Taking into consideration the fact that the two ladies could not agree fully on what they had seen, it is certainly possible that they projected their own imaginings upon the scene as they walked.

On the other hand, their description of features in the Versailles grounds accords closely with plans for proposed improvements drawn up in 1774 by the head gardener, Antoine Richard, although there is no firm evidence that these plans were ever realized. The possibility must be borne in mind, however, that during their stay in Paris the two ladies had seen a print of these plans, and had unconsciously remembered them.

Unfortunately, there is no record of the weather at Versailles on 10 August 1901. Both remarked upon the oppressive atmosphere and the 'flatness' of their surroundings, conditions that often presage the onset of a thundery storm. This is the 'warm and muggy' weather that parapsychologist T. C. Lethbridge and others have noted as particularly conducive to paranormal experiences. Setting aside the possibility that the 'adventure' was imaginary, there are two questions to be asked: were they the ghosts of Marie-Antoinette and members of Louis XVI's court that Miss Moberly and Miss Jourdain saw, or did the

GREG SHELDON MAXWELL

In 1992, two-year-old Greg Sheldon Maxwell began to exclaim 'Old Nana's here', and pointed up into the air in front of him. This photograph is claimed to show his great-grandmother's ghost appearing before him.

ladies both experience a 'slip in time', and somehow observe a real event that took place 110 years before?

THE HELPFUL GHOST

Place: Nogales, Arizona, USA

Time: 1942

Reporter: Gordon St Thomas

Gordon St Thomas, an officer of the US Immigration Service, was transferred to Nogales, on the border with Mexico, in 1942. He rented a former bachelor army officer's quarters, a long, one-storey house built during the 19th century, and moved in with his wife Sarah and two young children.

From the beginning, they often had the feeling that, when they entered a room, someone had just left it. Then St Thomas became aware that there was an entity about the house that seemed to be obsessed with tidiness. He would return home from duty and throw his cap on to a chair, only to find it, a minute or two later, hanging from a hook. If he left a book open upon a table, it would be replaced in the bookshelves. Packets of cigarettes lying around would end up in the wastebasket. One morning he left the coffee percolator on the stove with the gas turned up full beneath it and went to shave; when he remembered, several minutes later, and hurried back to the kitchen, he found the gas turned down low.

The most remarkable event, however, occurred one night when St Thomas came off duty late, and decided to sleep in a spare bedroom so as not to wake his wife. As he was falling asleep, he felt his foot shaken vigorously; sitting up, he switched on the light, but found the room empty. He was about to switch off the light again when, looking up, he saw a scorpion on the ceiling immediately over the bed. As surrounding temperatures fall at night, scorpions can feel the heat rising from a sleeping body, and move to it. St Thomas was convinced that the 'ghost' had saved his life by warning him about the scorpion.

COMMENTARY:

The fact that the house had previously been occupied by soldiers, during the border wars with Mexico and the pursuit of the Apache chief Geronimo, suggests that the ghost may well have been that of a military man, one of those renowned for their insistence on neatness and order. St Thomas is now dead; more than 70 years after his experiences, the exact location of the building has not been discovered, and so nothing is known of its previous history.

A GHOST IN GREENWICH VILLAGE

Place: 11 Bank Street, New York City, USA

Time: 1957

Reporter: Meyer Berger

The *New York Times* for 26 June 1957 contained a report, in Meyer Berger's column 'About New York', concerning a 'rather friendly' ghost who haunted the brownstone house of engineer Dr Harvey Slatin and his wife, painter Yeffe Kimball, at 11 Bank Street in Greenwich Village. The Slatins had acquired the premises from a Mrs Maccario, who had previously run it as a boarding house, but who, on subsequent questioning, was unable to furnish any particulars of previous occupants.

On numerous occasions, the Slatins had thought that they heard a woman's footsteps crossing the upper floors, and sometimes a sound like a faint hammering. They were not disturbed by the noises, although they frequently went in search of anything that might be causing them. The sounds occurred more often in the daytime than at night, and even the maid, after her initial fear, became accustomed to them.

A local carpenter, an Englishman named Arthur Brodie, who was brought in to carry out modifications on the 125-year-old house, maintained stolidly that 'one hears all sorts of noises in old houses'. Then, one morning in February 1957, he appeared at Mrs Slatin's bedroom door, exclaiming: 'It's me ma'am, I'm leaving the job! I've found the body!' – but he was only joking. Working on the ceiling of an upstairs room, he had dislodged a load of plaster, together with a japanned metal container, which had fallen to the floor. It bore the label of the United States Crematory Co., Queens, NY, with a faded inscription reading 'The last remains of Elizabeth Bullock, deceased, cremated January 21, 1931'. Curiously, the ceiling itself dated back to at least 1880.

Enquiries established that Elizabeth Bullock had been crossing nearby Hudson Street in January 1931 when she had been hit by a fast-moving car. Bystanders had carried her to a nearby drugstore, but she had died before an ambulance arrived. However, she had not lived at 11 Bank Street, but at 113 Perry Street.

Mrs Slatin was immediately reminded that, some weeks before, a well-dressed young man had called at the door and asked if any rooms were to let. He had left a card, with the name 'E. C. Bullock'.

COMMENTARY:

Self-styled 'ghost hunter' Hans Holzer read the story in the *New York Times*, and arranged a seance at the Slatin home on 17 July, bringing his friend and medium Mrs Ethel Meyers. As Mrs Meyers went into trance, she described a woman, 'Betty', who walked slowly, being paralyzed on one side, and who had a heart condition.

Speaking with the Irish-accented voice of 'Betty', Mrs Meyers said that she and her brother Eddie, who now lived in California, came from Pleasantville, New York State, and that their mother's maiden name had been Elizabeth McCuller. 'He didn't want me in the family plot – my brother – I wasn't even married in their eyes… but I was married before God… my husband went with Eddie… steal the ashes… pay for no burial… he came back and took them from Eddie… hide ashes… Charles knew it… made a roof over the house… ashes came through the roof… so Eddie can't find them… and I like being with you!', nodding towards Mrs Slatin.

Who arranged the cremation? 'It was Charles's wish, and it wasn't Eddie's and therefore they quarrelled. Charlie was a Presbyterian… and he would have put me in his church, but I could not offend them all. They put it beyond my reach through the roof; still hot… they stole it from the crematory.' Then Mrs Meyers relaxed, and emerged from her trance. Holzer suggested to Mrs Slatin that the can should be buried in the garden at the back of the house, but she felt that it should be put on the family's piano in the living room – and there it remained.

A MASS FOR THE DYING

Place: Beaulieu Abbey, Hampshire, England

Time: 1959

Reporters: Michael Sedgwick and the Hon. Elizabeth Varley

Beaulieu, seat of the Montagu family and the site of a motor museum, was one of the abbeys closed down in the 16th century during King Henry VIII's dissolution of the monasteries. Shortly before Christmas 1959, Michael Sedgwick, the curator of the museum, was working late one night in his cottage close by the ruined former chapel of the abbey. He had been smoking, and, on opening the window to clear the air, heard something very unusual:

The ruined cloisters at Beaulieu Abbey. The sound of monks chanting a Gregorian mass was heard by several people on at least two occasions when someone in the nearby village was dying.

'It was definitely chanting, and very beautiful chanting. It came in uneven waves, as if from a faulty wireless – sometimes quite loud and then fading away. It was just as if a Catholic mass was being played on the radio in the next flat, but I thought it was curious that anyone should have the radio on at that time of night. Anyway, it was so beautiful that I tried to find it on my own wireless... and I couldn't. Later I was told it was just a common-or-garden supernatural phenomenon.'

Sedgwick heard the chanting again, on another night when he was working unusually late. Renee Bartlett, wife of film director Fred Zinnemann, also reported hearing it, when some scenes for Zinnemann's film *A Man for All Seasons* were being shot at the abbey in 1965. A Montagu family member, the Hon. Elizabeth Susan Varley, confirmed that she heard the chanting on several occasions. The first time was when she was aged about 18, and living in another house in the abbey grounds.

'It was a hot summer's night, very late,' she said, 'and I was sitting on my window-seat, looking out... I was so deep in my thoughts that it had been going on for quite a while before I became conscious of it. What made me first aware of it was the frissons of cold that began to run up and down my back. It was the sound of many voices in repetitive singing, which faded and strengthened like the sound from a primitive wireless. At first I thought it was a wireless in the servants' hall. But the sound wasn't coming from there. I couldn't tell you where it was coming from. The next morning an archaeologist friend asked me to sing the tune to him. It was pretty well carved in my memory, so I sang it. He told me it was a well-known Gregorian chant.'

COMMENTARY:

Michael Sedgwick later reported that he had discovered that on two occasions he had heard the chanting on the night that someone in the village had died. This was confirmed by a former catering manager at Beaulieu, Mrs Bertha Day, who also heard the singing. And others, including Lord Montagu himself, had sometimes noticed the strong – and inexplicable – smell of incense.

Many old establishments such as Beaulieu Abbey have stories of ghostly monks attached to them, but few, if any, offer such well-attested phenomena from objective observers.

THE PHANTOMS OF FLIGHT 401

Place: Aircraft of Eastern Airlines, USA

Time: From 1972 onwards

Early in December 1972, a stewardess with Eastern Airlines told some of her colleagues of a premonition in which she had seen a Lockheed TriStar on approach to Miami International Airport. She saw the port wing crumple as the aircraft hit the ground, and heard the despairing cries of the injured. The disaster would occur, she said, 'around the holidays, closer to New Year'. Asked if she and her colleagues were to be the cabin crew, she replied: 'No, but it's going to be real close'.

On 29 December, there was a last-minute change in crew schedules: the stewardess and her colleagues did not take Flight 401 from New York to Miami. Late in the evening, that aircraft crashed in the Florida Everglades, with several of the flight crew and many of the passengers being killed. Among the fatalities were Captain Bob Loft and the flight engineer, Second Officer Don Repo.

The cause of the crash was found to be a couple of minor design faults in the controls, and Lockheed quickly corrected them. However, it appears that some undamaged parts of the aircraft were

Captain Robert Loft of Eastern Airlines Flight 401. On 29 December 1972, the New York to Miami flight that he was piloting crashed in the Florida Everglades, causing many fatalities.

Second Officer Don Repo of Flight 401. After their deaths, several Eastern Airlines cabin crew reported seeing Loft and Repo on other flights, sometimes issuing warnings that became true.

subsequently recycled in other planes. Following this, a number of mysterious incidents were reported.

One of the vice-presidents of Eastern Airlines boarded a Miami-bound TriStar at JFK airport, and spoke to a uniformed captain sitting in First Class. Suddenly he recognized that the captain was Bob Loft – at which point the apparition vanished. On another occasion at JFK, Loft was seen, and spoken to, by the plane's captain and two flight attendants. The captain was sufficiently disturbed to cancel the flight.

One aircraft, numbered 318, was particularly affected. A woman found herself sitting next to an Eastern Airlines flight officer who looked pale and ill, but would not speak; she called a

stewardess but, before the eyes of several people, the man disappeared. The woman was later shown photographs of Eastern Airlines engineers, and identified the late Don Repo. On another flight, from New York to Mexico City, Repo's face appeared in the oven window, and two stewardesses and an engineer from the flight deck heard him say: 'Watch out for fire on this airplane'. On its take-off from Mexico City, one of the plane's engines malfunctioned, and it had to return to the airport.

There were other incidents. A male voice on the PA announced the seat-belt and no-smoking precautions, when the PA had not been switched on and none of the crew had made the announcement. A flight engineer making the pre-flight checks found a man in a second officer's uniform, whom he recognized as Repo, sitting at the control panel. The apparition said 'You don't need to worry about the pre-flight, I've already done it,' and vanished. One TriStar captain said that he had also spoken to Repo, who told him: 'There will never be another crash [of a TriStar]… we will not let it happen'.

COMMENTARY:

These, and many other incidents, were investigated by John G. Fuller in his book *The Ghost of Flight 401*. It is an unusually detailed case of 'protective' ghosts. It is as if the trauma of the crash, which was in part due to the fact that the flight crew were unaware of the design faults and inadvertently over-rode some of the automatic controls, preyed so heavily on the dead officers' spirits that they had to watch over the subsequent fate of the aircraft in which the recycled pieces had been incorporated. Fuller also claimed to have contacted Repo by means of a Ouija board.

An inflated life raft can be seen lying in front of the scattered debris of the Lockheed TriStar Flight 401 in the Florida Everglades in 1972.

ON SACRED GROUND

Place: Thorpe Park, Surrey, England

Time: 2011

One might have thought that hauntings would never be allowed to get in the way of big business, but that was not the case in 2011 when the Thorpe Park theme park in Surrey changed its building plans to appease the dead.

Building work had begun on a new water ride called Storm Surge, which would cross Monk's Walk, an old footpath that has linked the ruins of nearby Chertsey Abbey to Thorpe Church since 666 AD. But staff soon reported paranormal experiences, including seeing a headless monk, sensing that someone was watching them, finding that objects had been moved and experiencing sudden cold feelings.

To build the new ride, foundations would be dug 15 metres (50 feet) down into an area where stone coffins had earlier been excavated.

With the staff unnerved by the paranormal experiences, management called in Jim Arnold of South West London Paranormal. 'Results were picked up immediately,' said Arnold, with orbs, ghostly images in photography and Ouija reaction results being strongest around the site where the park was proposing to build Storm Surge. 'The results were so strong, we felt the only explanation could be that an ancient burial ground or settlement was being disturbed, prompting the extra paranormal activity.'

Forensic geophysicist Peter Masters, of Cranfield University, Bedfordshire, used radar to analyse the site and found 'signatures similar to that of a burial ground'. In the interest of keeping the spirits quiet and its staff happy, management moved the site of Storm Surge over to another part of the park.

COMMENTARY:

Building on ancient burial grounds, disturbing the dead and being haunted as a consequence is a popular motif in fiction and movies about ghosts, such as *Poltergeist* (1982), among others. But that is

what spooked the planners at Thorpe Park. And it didn't take much: the disturbances were relatively mild, but the management took them seriously enough to move the ride to another area of the park. Since the ride opened in 2011, there have been no further reports of any ghost sightings.

When work began on the foundations of a new ride at Thorpe Park, staff reported paranormal experiences, including seeing a headless monk.

CHAPTER 5

SOME MALIGN PRESENCE

Although apparitions usually behave as if unaware of the people who see them, some haunting entities appear to be driven by a kind of malevolent intelligence. Many of the phenomena resemble poltergeist attacks and some are even life-threatening.

WITCHCRAFT IN SALEM

Place: Salem (now Danvers), Massachusetts, USA

Time: 1692

The events at Salem have become one of the most famous incidents in early American history, because they led to accusations of witchcraft and a notorious trial. In their early manifestation, however, they showed many of the typical signs that in later centuries came to be identified with certain types of poltergeist activity.

It began at the end of December 1691, when seven young girls of Salem, Essex County, were whiling away the time with an 'oracle' consisting of an egg poured into a wine glass. Their plan was to discover who their future husbands were to be, and they had been instructed in this method of fortune-telling by Tituba, the Barbadian slave of the Rev. Samuel Parris. The outcome, however, was not at all what they expected. Rev. Parris's nine-year-old daughter Elizabeth, and his 11-year-old niece Abigail Williams, were thrown into hysterical fits, followed shortly by the other girls: 12-year-old Ann Putnam, and four others: Elizabeth Hubbard, Mary Walcott, Mary Warren and Mercy Lewis, with ages ranging from 16 to 20.

'Their motion in their fits,' wrote Rev. Deodat Lawson, 'are preternatural, both as to the manner, which is so strange as a well person could not screw their body into; and as to the violence… it is much beyond the ordinary force of the same person when they are in their right mind.'

Rev. Parris, sensibly, removed his daughter and niece to the home of a friend some miles away, but the other girls remained in Salem. They began to see

The Château of Champtocé in Anjou, France was the birthplace of Gilles de Rais. He is reputed to have killed between 140 and 200 children. His ghostly spirit still broods over Champtocé.

The Ingersoll Tavern in Salem, scene of the preliminary hearings of the witchcraft trials. The accusations of witchcraft followed the sightings of 'spectral figures' by girls aged between nine and 20.

'spectral figures', which they said struck, scratched and beat them, often leaving marks on their flesh. The doctor, William Griggs, pronounced: 'The Evil Hand is upon them.' In February 1692, the girls named their tormentors: Tituba the slave, and two elderly, unpopular members of the community, Sarah Good and Sarah Osburne. Soon they were accusing more and more people – eventually even the wife of Governor Phips of Massachusetts and the president of Harvard.

This is not the place to describe the panic that seized the people of Salem, nor the trials for witchcraft that resulted in the death of 20 villagers and the arrest of another 200. Phips, who was absent from the colony during the summer of 1692, returned in October, and gradually restored order. The Salem magistrates publicly admitted their errors – but nothing could ever atone for the death or distress of so many innocent persons.

COMMENTARY:

The violent reaction to the 'possession' of the girls followed on from the great witchcraft purges that had taken place in Europe earlier in the century. The colonists, many of them first-generation immigrants, felt insecure in their new home, threatened on all sides by the possibility of attack by Native Americans, and deeply suspicious of the strange religious practices of their slaves. Pious Puritans as they were, the possibility that the Devil had come among them woke all their superstitious fears.

In such an emotional climate, the inexplicable nature of the girls' seizures was enough to support the accusation of witchcraft. With the evidence we now have of poltergeist phenomena, the fact that the girls were all of premenstrual or pubescent age is highly significant. Commentators have disagreed on whether they suffered a genuine hysterical disturbance, or whether they were consciously practising a vicious deceit, but whatever the case, the events in Salem cast some illumination upon the cases that follow.

THE BELL WITCH

Place: Robertson County, Tennessee, USA

Time: 1817–1820

Victims: John Bell, his wife Luce and children

The haunting began with knocking and scraping on the outside of the Bell house in Robertson County, Tennessee. In it lived John Bell, a farmer, his wife Luce, and nine children, including John Jr, Joel, Drewry, Betsy, 12, and Richard, six. Later the noises entered the house, becoming louder: gnawing on bedposts, flapping on the ceiling, sounds of chairs being toppled, heavy chains dragged across the floor. Then both Richard and Betsy (in separate rooms) were awakened one night by something pulling at their hair. Betsy's face was slapped, leaving bright crimson patches.

Sticks and stones were thrown at the Bell children as they went to school. The violence increased: people were struck in the face by what felt like a clenched fist. Then Betsy began to suffer from fainting fits, after each of which a voice was heard, at first faint and inarticulate, then a low but distinct whisper. It named itself the Witch. It repeated, word for word, the Sunday sermons of two local parsons, imitating their voices. Soon it began to utter obscenities, announced its hatred for 'old Jack Bell', and declared it would torment him for the rest of his life.

Some neighbours suggested that Betsy herself might be producing the voice of the Witch, but the local doctor, placing his hand over Betsy's mouth, 'soon satisfied himself that she was in no way connected with these sounds'.

John Bell began to complain of something punching both sides of his jaw: his tongue became so swollen that he could not speak or eat. He developed a nervous tic, and took to his bed, where he lay constantly twitching. At the same time Luce was showered with gifts of fruit and nuts, which appeared from nowhere; but Joel, Drewry and Richard were frequently struck.

After three years, Betsy, now 15, became engaged to a neighbour, Joshua Gardner, but the Witch repeatedly whispered in her ear: 'Please, Betsy Bell, don't have Joshua Gardner, please, Betsy Bell, don't marry him.' The engagement was broken off.

That autumn, John Bell roused himself, and attempted to attend to his farm, but Richard reported how his father was struck a heavy blow on the head and fell at the roadside, while 'the reviling sound of derisive songs and demoniac shrieks' echoed all around them.

John Bell retired once more to his bed, and on the morning of 19 December 1820 he was found in a deep stupor, from which he could not be roused. The doctor was summoned, but the Witch could be heard crying: 'It's useless for you to try and revive old Jack – I have got him this time. He will never get up from that bed again.' He died the following morning. At the funeral, as his coffin was lowered into the grave, the Witch's voice could be heard singing a vulgar song: 'Row me up some brandy, O'.

Little was heard of the Witch after this. One night, a voice was heard announcing that it was leaving, but would return after seven years. It did so, when only Luce, Joel and Richard were left in the house, but produced no more than a short scuffling and pulling of bedclothes.

COMMENTARY:

Psychologist Nandor Fodor made a study of this case in 1951, based partly on Richard Bell's account of his family's trauma in *Our Family Trouble*. He pointed out that Betsy's fainting fits were not unlike the phenomenon of a medium going into trance, and the girl was of an age frequently associated with poltergeist activity.

John Bell, on the other hand, wrote Fodor, showed all the symptoms of acute guilt complex. Noting that the onset of puberty could be traumatic in the environment in which Betsy was raised, Fodor made a 'purely speculative guess' that the experience might have triggered the awakening of long-suppressed memories. His theory was, he said, 'not for the grim and prudish': he suggested that Betsy might have been molested by her father in childhood.

Fodor's conclusion was that Betsy had suffered a split in her personality, and that in some unexplained way part of her subconscious had taken on a life of its own, which steadily drove her father to his death.

A ROMANIAN DEVIL

Place: Buhai, Romania

Time: 1925–1927

Victim: Eleonora Zugun

One of the most intensively investigated cases of 'possession' by a supernatural force is that of Eleonora Zugun. She was a peasant girl born in the village of Talpa, in northern Romania, on 24 May

A photograph from a film made by Harry Price of the Romanian girl Eleonora Zugun. The stigmata on her cheek, like vicious scratches and welts, appeared spontaneously during filming.

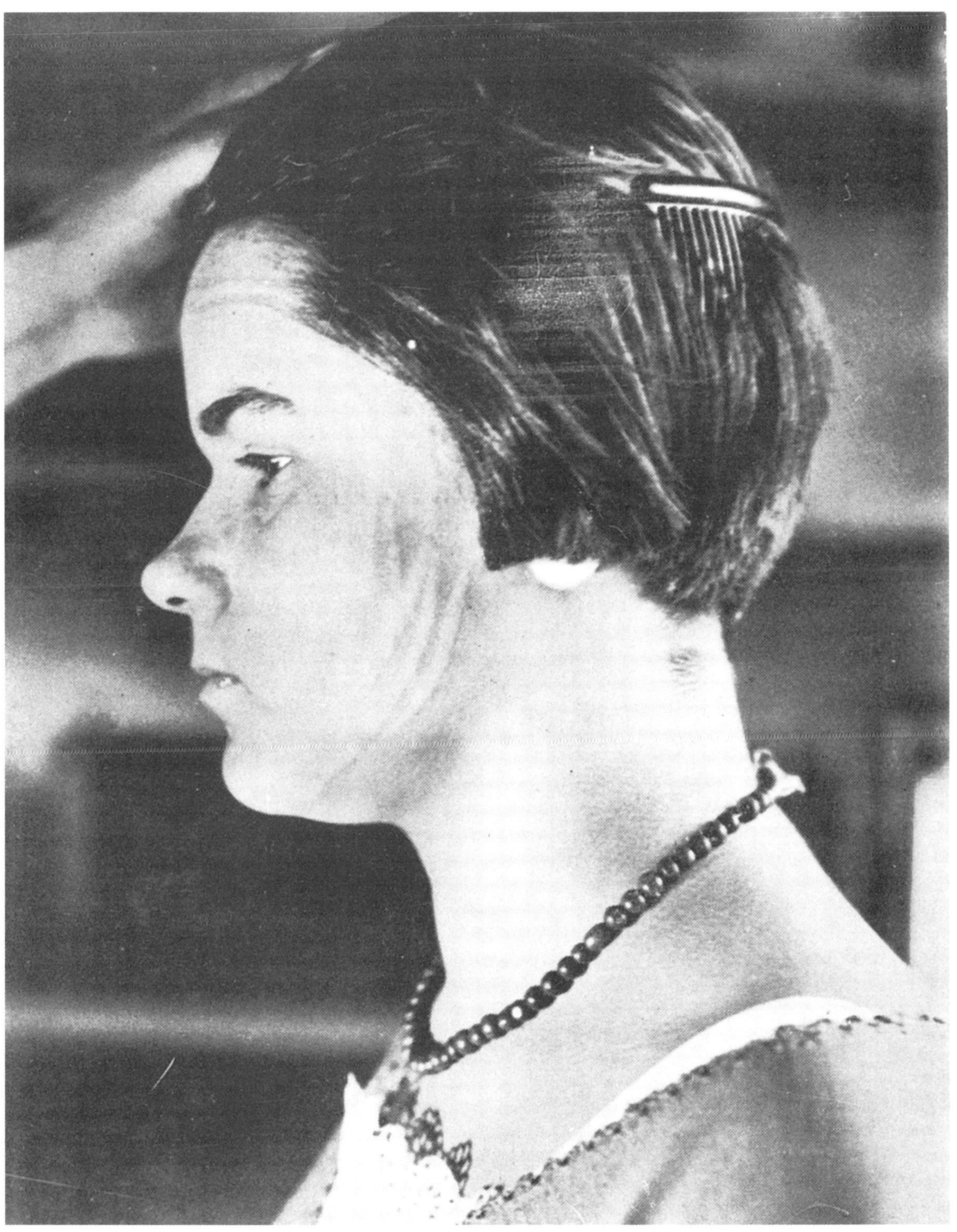

Psychical researcher Harry Price. Although doubts have been cast on some of Price's methods, the photographs and film that he took of Eleonora Zugun have so far defied a non-ghostly explanation.

1913, and at the age of 12 she was sent to stay with her grandparents in the village of Buhai. One day, it is said, she found some money lying at the roadside, and used it to buy sweets. But when she told her grandmother the old lady flew into a rage, declaring that the money had been left there by malicious spirits.

The next day, a shower of stones was hurled at the cottage, breaking several windows, and this was followed by a piece of china and a half-brick. Inside the house, an iron ring fell from the stove, and a mug from the dresser. Convinced that the girl, on eating the ill-gotten sweets, had become infected with a *dracu* (devil), her grandparents sent Eleonora back home to Talpa.

But the phenomena continued. As the family sat eating a meal at their kitchen table, a stone crashed through the window. It was wet, and appeared to have come from the River Seret, a few yards away. The village priest was sent for. He marked the stone with a cross, and tossed it back into the river. A few minutes later the same stone, still marked, flew again into the house.

After several days of like events, Eleonora's father decided to take her to an old man called Macarescu, the priest of nearby Zamostea. As soon as Eleonora entered his room, an iron vessel burst into pieces, followed by an earthenware pot. The local schoolteacher watched in amazement as a can of water placed at the end of a bench was raised 45cm (18 inches) into the air, turned through a half-circle, and set down at the other end of the bench, without a drop being spilled. When someone suggested a pilgrimage to the shrine of St Johannes at Suczava, a stone was hurled against a picture of the saint that hung on the wall, destroying it.

In despair, Eleonora's parents sent her to the convent of Gorovei. Priests said masses for her; she was exorcised; investigators came from Chernivtsi University in Ukraine – but to no avail. Eventually the girl was declared insane, and incarcerated in the local asylum. Inevitably, the case was reported in the newspapers, and attracted the attention of the Berlin engineer and psychic researcher Fritz Grünewald. He was able to persuade Eleonora's father to withdraw her from the asylum and return her to the convent, where he kept her under observation for several weeks, and saw numerous inexplicable phenomena. Grünewald made arrangements to transfer Eleonora to a private home near Berlin, where he could continue his investigations, but before this could be done he died of a heart attack.

Fortunately, Countess Zo Wassilko-Serecki, a Romanian interested in psychic research, came to the rescue. She took Eleonora to live with her in Vienna, and in May 1926 the English psychic investigator Harry Price met the girl for the first time:

'I found Eleonora to be an intelligent, well-developed, bright girl with a sunny disposition… Though physically strong and healthy, she was "young" mentally. In many ways she was more like a girl of eight: her shyness; her extreme fondness for simple toys; her simple games and childish ways. But she could read and write well and was even something of an artist… The Countess and I seated ourselves on a couch and watched Eleonora playing with a toy that fascinated her… The girl ran to the countess and asked her to mend it. As I watched my hostess examining the join, a steel stiletto with handle, used for opening letters, shot across the room from behind me and fell against the closed door. I instantly turned round and a minute investigation revealed nothing – and no one – that could have projected the stiletto, which was normally kept on the writing table behind us, against the wall farthest from where we stood.'

During his stay in Vienna, Price witnessed many similar phenomena. He also discovered that Eleonora had begun to exhibit stigmata: scratches and welts – on one occasion as many as 25 – on her face, neck and arms. She attributed these marks to attacks by the *dracu*. The countess wrote in her diary that she had watched them emerge, 'exactly as though she had been bitten by somebody', even while she held the girl's hands. Price invited the countess and Eleonora to his laboratory in the University of London.

For more than three weeks in 1926, Price and a succession of scientists observed Eleonora in London. The phenomena were not numerous, but remained inexplicable: coins were dislodged from a high shelf; a letter L intended for use with a magnetic noticeboard, and which was kept in a closed box in a cupboard in the library, fell from the air on to the child's head; and another letter, C, was found by Dr R. J. Tillyard, a scientist from Rothamsted Research Station, wedged around the clasp of a small case containing his penknife, which he kept in his coat pocket.

During the visit, the stigmata appeared regularly while Eleonora was under close observation, and Price was able to obtain a graphic series of photographs, including a filmed record, as they emerged. The countess and the girl returned to Vienna on 24 October, and he did not see them again. However, he learnt a few months later that Eleonora had begun to menstruate, and that, almost overnight, all phenomena ceased.

COMMENTARY:

Price's detailed notes, his photographs, and in particular his film, have made this one of the most closely studied cases. He was fortunate in being able to call on the assistance of leading psychologists, as well as seasoned investigators from the Society for Psychical Research. Eleonora also attracted the attention of the British press, whose representatives were considerably impressed.

In many ways this is a typical poltergeist case, and the phenomena duly ceased as the girl entered puberty. As always, suspicions were voiced that everything was attributable to trickery, that the girl herself was physically moving objects, throwing them, hiding them. Price, however, was confident that he had kept close control of conditions, and that trickery was out of the question.

Eleonora attributed the phenomena, and particularly the stigmata, to the activities of her *dracu*. No doubt the fear associated with this belief heightened the emotional tension of early adolescence that appears to be connected with poltergeist activity. Spontaneous stigmata of this kind are often encountered in people in a condition of ecstasy; the physiological cause is unknown, but there is more than a passing resemblance to some of the symptoms of nervous psoriasis.

GHOST AND DIVINING ROD

Place: Branscombe, Devon, England

Time: 1959–1962

Reporter: T. C. Lethbridge

In the autumn of 1957, T. C. Lethbridge, a recently retired archaeologist, and his wife Mina moved into the 14th-century Hole House at Branscombe, on the south coast of Devon. The experience they had there is of particular interest in view of the theory that Lethbridge developed as a result.

One of his near neighbours, at Hole Mill, was an eccentric but friendly old lady who had the local reputation of being a witch. On 22 February 1959, Lethbridge was sitting on the hillside above the old lady's house when he saw her with another woman, dressed in a dark skirt with a wide-brimmed hat – a style of dress that reminded him of the clothes worn by his aunts before World War I. A few minutes later, he and Mina strolled down to their neighbour's gate, and asked after her visitor. 'Ah,' said the old lady, 'you're seeing my ghosts now.'

At this time, Lethbridge was planning his book *Ghosts and Ghouls* (1961), and he decided to see whether the ghost would reappear at the same time the following year. He and Mina waited expectantly, but saw nothing, although they agreed that they had both felt 'an electric tingling in the air'.

Three years passed and then, one day in January 1962, the Lethbridges drove to a nearby bay to collect seaweed to fertilize their garden. 'As I stepped on to the beach,' Lethbridge later wrote, 'I passed into a kind of blanket or fog of depression and, I think, fear.' A few minutes later Mina came hurrying back from along the beach: 'I can't stand this place any longer,' she said. 'There's something frightful here… '

A few days after this, the couple returned to the beach: 'the same bank of depression greeted me at the same place as before', wrote Lethbridge. It appeared to be centred on a spot where a small stream ran down to the sea. At the spot where Mina had experienced her disturbing feeling the week before, 'the feeling was at its worst. It was so strong as to make me feel almost giddy. The nearest I can get to a description is that it felt not unlike one feels with a high temperature and when full of drugs. There was definitely a feeling of tingling to accompany it.' The couple returned to the cliff top, and here Mina experienced a sensation as if someone were urging her to jump from it.

COMMENTARY:

The old neighbour had died during the previous year, after threatening to put a spell upon a local farmer, and Lethbridge noticed that an unpleasant

Branscombe in East Devon, where T. C. Lethbridge experienced an unusual 'fog of depression'. He went on to develop a theory that running water, such as underground streams, could carry impressions of emotional events.

feeling had also seemed to linger around her house. He began to put his various experiences together: the weather, 'warm and muggy', that had prevailed on each occasion; the feelings of depression and weakness associated with certain spots; and the tingling sensation that accompanied them.

Lethbridge had for years been practising the art of dowsing for water, and his conversations with the old lady had quickened his interest. At the spot on the hillside from where he had seen the dark-clad ghost, a stream disappeared below ground. With his dowser's rod Lethbridge was able to trace its course: it curved, and ran directly below the place where the figure had stood.

In *Ghost and Divining Rod* (1963), Lethbridge put forward his theory that the running water created a force field not unlike that surrounding a cable carrying electric current – which can often also produce a 'tingling' sensation in those who go close to it. This field, he suggested, could in some way carry an impression – a 'recording' – of the emotional events that had occurred within it. (At the very least, this theory went some way towards explaining how water-divining 'worked'.)

Using a pendulum rather than a divining rod, Lethbridge investigated the fields surrounding other materials, and came up with what might appear at first to be an over-fanciful proposition. The ancients, he said, had identified the 'spirits' of the landscape: naiads in running water, dryads in woodland, oreads among the rocks. What if this were evidence of their awareness of these force fields, which they then attributed to supernatural powers, as they did thunder and lightning? A considerable part of the rest of Lethbridge's life was devoted to investigating the matter. One piece of information certainly helped Lethbridge to strengthen his belief in his force fields: the cliff where Mina had felt the temptation to jump, above where the stream ran into the sea, proved to be the spot where a man had committed suicide some years before.

WHAT HAPPENED AT AMITYVILLE?

Place: Amityville, Long Island, USA

Time: 1975–1976

Reporters: George and Kathy Lutz, Jay Anson

A large house in Dutch Colonial style, built in 1928, stands on Ocean Avenue, in Amityville, Long Island. On the morning of 13 November 1974, one of the sons of the family who owned it, Ronald DeFeo, ran into a nearby bar, screaming that someone had broken into the house and slaughtered his parents, two brothers and two sisters. The state had little difficulty in proving that Ronald himself had shot all six – possibly hoping to profit from a life insurance policy worth $200,000 – and he was sentenced to six consecutive terms of life imprisonment.

The house remained empty for more than a year before it was bought by George and Kathy Lutz, who moved in with their three children on 18 December 1975. A month later they left, never to return. The story of their experiences was first told by George Lutz in an article in the *Long Island Press* on 17 January 1976, and subsequently in the April 1977 issue of *Good Housekeeping*. Finally, the story was told in Jay Anson's book, *The Amityville Horror* (1978), and was the subject of two successful films (*The Amityville Horror,* made in 1979, and a remake in 2005), as well as numerous sequels and prequels.

Anson based his tale on numerous interviews conducted with the Lutz family. According to their account, the trouble began with foul odours that filled the house, black slime in the bathroom, and hundreds of flies that invaded a bedroom. The heavy front door to the house was found wrenched open and hanging from a single hinge. Tracks of cloven hooves were seen in the snow, and the garage door was found almost torn away, with 'a strength far beyond that of any human being'.

Kathy Lutz reported that she felt invisible arms encircling her, from which she was unable to escape, and red weals appeared on her body. George Lutz reported the sound of an invisible band marching through the house, with blaring brass and thundering footsteps. Later, he described seeing Kathy levitating above their bed on several occasions, and reported the appearance of an entity variously described as a gigantic hooded white figure, and a horned demon with half of its face shot away. And when their little daughter pointed one night at the window, George and Kathy saw 'two fiery red eyes. No face, just the mean little eyes of a pig', while Kathy screamed: 'It's been here all the time. I wanted to kill it!'

COMMENTARY:

Even from the beginning, local opinion was that the Lutz family had greatly exaggerated their experiences. The police denied ever having been asked to investigate the terrifying occurrences, and local handymen said they knew nothing of any damage to the premises. After months of investigation, Dr Stephen Kaplan, then director of

The house at Amityville as it was portrayed in the 1979 film *The Amityville Horror*. The real house had been the site of a family mass killing and remained empty for more than a year before the Lutz family moved in.

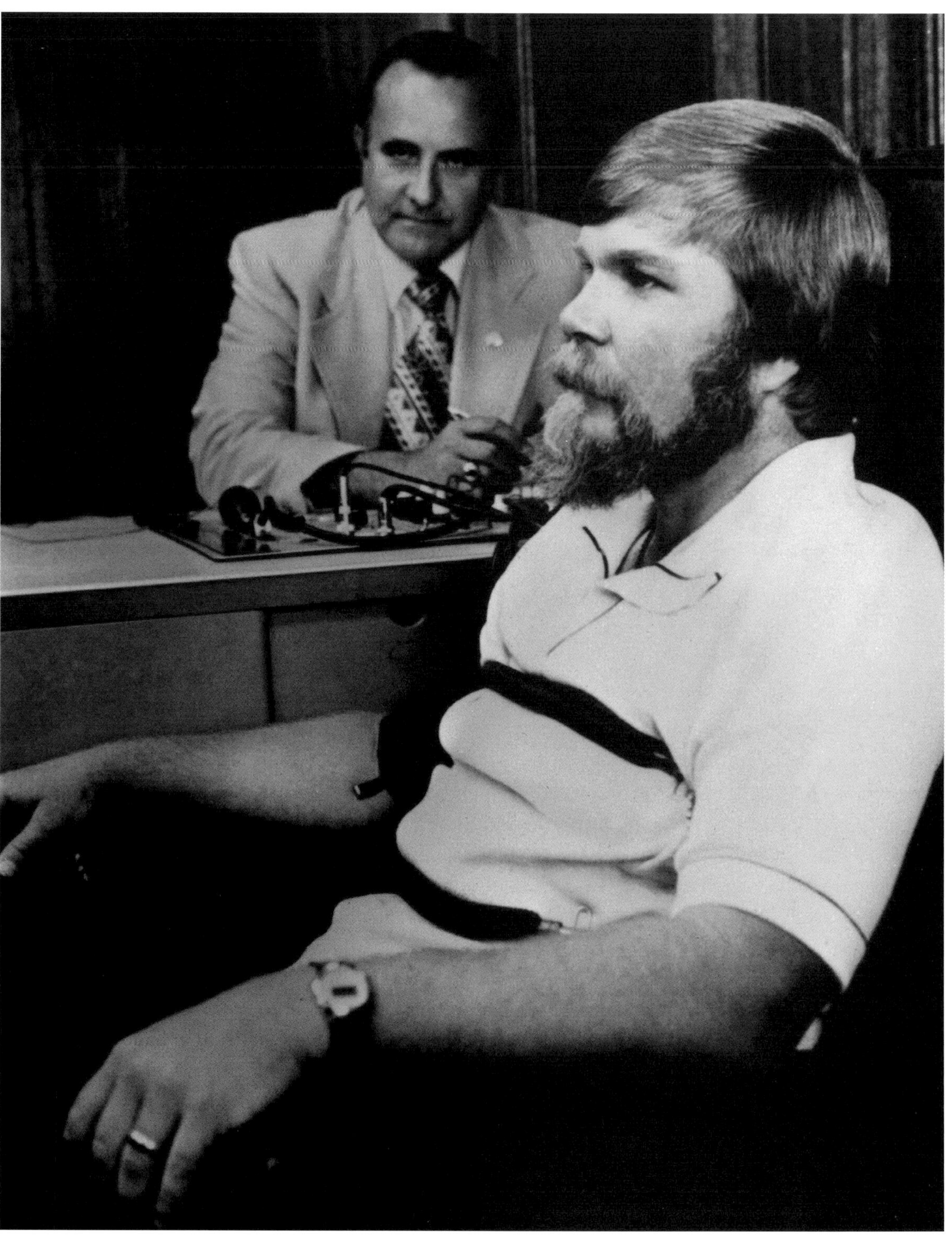

It was the opinion of the Parapsychology Institute of America that George Lutz (pictured), whose family had moved into the Amityville house, had made up the increasingly heightened reports of a haunting.

the Parapsychology Institute of America, delivered his opinion of the case: 'We found no evidence to support any claim of a "haunted house". What we did find was a couple who had purchased a house that they could economically not afford. It is our professional opinion that the story of its haunting is mostly fiction.'

This view is supported by what is known of George Lutz's situation. This was his second marriage, and he was already facing difficulties before he moved to Amityville: Kathy's two sons had threatened to run away, his construction business was in difficulties, and he was in trouble over tax arrears. As Anson's book put it:

'He lay awake at night, worrying about: a second marriage with three children, a new house with a big mortgage. The taxes in Amityville were three times higher than in Deer Park. Did he really need that new speedboat? How the hell was he going to pay for all this?'

Between its appearances in the *Long Island Press*, *Good Housekeeping*, and *The Amityville Horror*, the story underwent many dramatic developments. It has been suggested that George Lutz persuaded himself that he was the physical and mental double of Ronald DeFeo, and gradually became obsessed by these morbid fantasies, embroidering the tale at every telling. It appears that it was DeFeo's defence attorney, William Weber, who was responsible for much of the publicity that was given to the story. His client had spoken of a voice urging him to kill his family, and Weber hoped to obtain a retrial by establishing that the house harboured some supernatural entity. As he said in a press release on 27 July 1979: 'We created this horror story over many bottles of wine that George was drinking. We were really playing with each other.'

A FIERY PRESENCE IN BEVERLY HILLS

Place: Beverly Hills, California, USA

Time: 1964–1967

Reporter: Joe Hyams

In the early months of 1964, journalist Joe Hyams and his wife, at that time the rising young film actress Elke Sommer, moved into a charming low-built house in Beverly Hills. Some time later, on 6 July, Elke was visited by journalist Edith Dahlfeld, who asked her, as they sat down to talk, if she was to be introduced to 'the man'. Thinking that it must be Joe who was referred to, Elke went in search of him, but could find him nowhere in the house.

The journalist described him: a huskily built man with a large 'potato' nose, dressed in dark trousers, and a white shirt with a black tie – quite unlike Joe Hyams. Discussing the matter later that day, the couple finally dismissed it as 'one of those inexplicable things you shrug off and forget'.

Two weeks later, however, Sommer's mother, who was visiting them, woke in the night to find a man at the foot of her bed, staring down at her. He disappeared before she could cry out, and in the morning Joe persuaded her that she probably had seen a night prowler at the window. However, examining the ground below her window, which rain in the night had made quite soft, he could find no trace of any footprints.

Then the couple began to hear strange noises, almost every night: sounds as if the chairs in the dining room were being pushed about. Later, while his wife was filming abroad, Hyams continued to hear the noises, and also found windows open that he had bolted the night before. Mystified, he bought three miniature radio transmitters and attached them to tape recorders. He concealed one at the entrance to the house driveway, one near the front door, and the third in the dining room itself.

That night, as he lay upstairs in bed, he heard once more the movement of the chairs. Picking up a revolver, he crept downstairs and along the hall to the dining room door, which he had purposely left open. With the gun in one hand, he switched on the lights. There was nobody in the room, and the chairs stood exactly where he had previously marked their positions with chalk.

In the morning, he played back his tapes. There were no unusual sounds recorded from the driveway or the front door – but in the dining room the transmitter had faithfully recorded the noises of the moving furniture, which stopped at the click of the light switch, his hesitant cough, and finally the sound of the chairs moving again once he had returned to bed.

For more than a year, guests in the house reported having caught glimpses of the thickset man in his white shirt and black tie. The house was searched from top to bottom, in case there was a nook where someone could hide himself, or a gap where he could have entered. There was nothing, and geologists assured Hyams that there was no evidence of ground movement that might have caused the noises. A detective hired to watch the house while the couple was away reported that locked doors and windows were found mysteriously opened, and the lights were often switched on and off.

Then the Hyams' pet dogs began behaving oddly, staring into the empty dining room and barking. Hyams enlisted the help of the Los Angeles branch of the American Society for Psychical Research (ASPR), and several scientists from UCLA also took an interest.

The ASPR sent a succession of, as Hyams put it, 'serious and I believe, with few exceptions, honest' mediums, who were told nothing of the house and its occupants' disturbing experiences. One reported the presence of a heavy-set man, a European; two described a large man of about 58 who had died of heart disease. One of these added that he had died 'before completing a task with the man of the house' – and Hyams recalled that a few years earlier he had been working on a book with a doctor who was in fact of that age, and who had died of a heart attack before the book was finished. Another described a 'monster', full of hate, and 'quite drunk'.

Hyams discovered that two previous occupants of the house had left it within months, declaring that it was haunted. He then asked the ASPR to arrange for one of the mediums, Mrs Lotte von Strahl, to come and 'lay' the ghost. Seated at the head of the dining room table, Mrs von Strahl announced that the 'horrible brutal monster' was beside her. She then asked Elke Sommer to join her in a short prayer, and proclaimed triumphantly, 'He's leaving.' That night Joe and Elke locked all the doors and windows, and retired to bed – only to hear, once more, the sound of the chairs moving in the dining room.

Hyams wrote an account of his paranormal experiences for the *Saturday Evening Post*, and declared: 'Even I am reluctantly convinced that we have at least one ghost in the house, but we don't intend to move out... I would not let a living man frighten me out of my house, and I certainly don't intend to let a dead one do it.'

Eight months later, however, he was forced to change his mind. In the early hours of 13 March

Actress Elke Sommer moved into a house in Beverly Hills in 1964 and for the next three years she, her husband and guests experienced paranormal activity, including seeing shadowy figures, hearing strange noises and finding locked windows opened.

WHITBY ABBEY

The stark ruins of Whitby Abbey, North Yorkshire, above the beach where, in Bram Stoker's novel *Dracula,* the vampire comes ashore. The ghost of Lady Hilda, who founded the abbey, is said to appear wrapped in a shroud in one of the ruin's high windows.

1967, Joe and Elke were awakened by a loud knocking on their bedroom door, and thought they heard laughter from downstairs. Opening the door, Joe found thick smoke billowing up. The couple hastily escaped from the bedroom window and down a sloping roof, and found the dining room furiously burning.

Arson investigators reported that the fire had 'mysterious origins'. Joe Hyams gave in, and put the house up for sale.

COMMENTARY:

Hyams became convinced that the fire had been started by the haunting presence, but another interpretation can be placed upon the event. At one time, Elke Sommer was convinced that the apparition was that of her dead father. If it was, the banging on the bedroom door that alerted the couple to their danger could have been a benevolent warning: it alerted them to the fire and they escaped.

JAPANESE GHOSTS

Stories of ghosts may be more numerous in the British Isles than anywhere else, but the Japanese are close rivals.

In some ways the ancient Japanese religion of Shinto can be compared to other major religions in that it promulgates the belief that, after death, human spirits are destined for an existence in eternity; and that there is also a purgatorial region, a half-world from which unhappy phantoms are able to return to earth with the purpose of haunting the living, to wreak their vengeance on those who harmed them while they were alive. Shinto, therefore, has developed a wealth of rituals – incorrectly regarded by westerners as 'ancestor worship' – the true purpose of which is rather to appease the spirits of the dead and to prevent their reappearance among the living.

Shinto is an early animistic religion in which animals, plants and inanimate objects are believed to possess a spiritual essence. The religion has contributed many stories to folklore; a prominent feature of these stories is the malignancy of the phantoms and the viciousness with which they attack their victims. With the coming of Buddhism to Japan, and the gradual modification of the original Shinto beliefs, the sheer maliciousness of these ghosts was explained in the concept that they sprang, not from purgatory, but from Hell itself.

One story, reputedly true, tells of the wicked lord Hotta Kozuke, who oppressed his subjects in the province of Soma with unfair taxes. The peasants decided to call in the assistance of the Shogun, and a brave village chief named Sakura Sogoro volunteered to deliver their petition. But the Shogun merely sent word to Kozuke to tell him what had occurred. The tyrannical lord forced Sogoro and his wife to watch while their three sons were beheaded, and then had the parents crucified. As he hung dying, Sogoro swore that he would return to haunt Kozuke to his dying day.

Among the most popular of Japanese ghost stories, perpetuated in several *kabuki* plays (a form of traditional drama that takes a well-known plot and develops it in a variety of versions), is that of the 18th-century samurai Aoyama Tessan, who fell in love with one of his servants, the beautiful Okiku. She, however, repulsed his advances, and he decided to trick her into compliance.

Tessan possessed a set of 10 valuable dishes, which were Okiku's special responsibility. He hid one away, and then asked Okiku to show him all 10. She produced them, but, of course, could account for only nine, although she counted them over and over. Tessan promised that she would not be

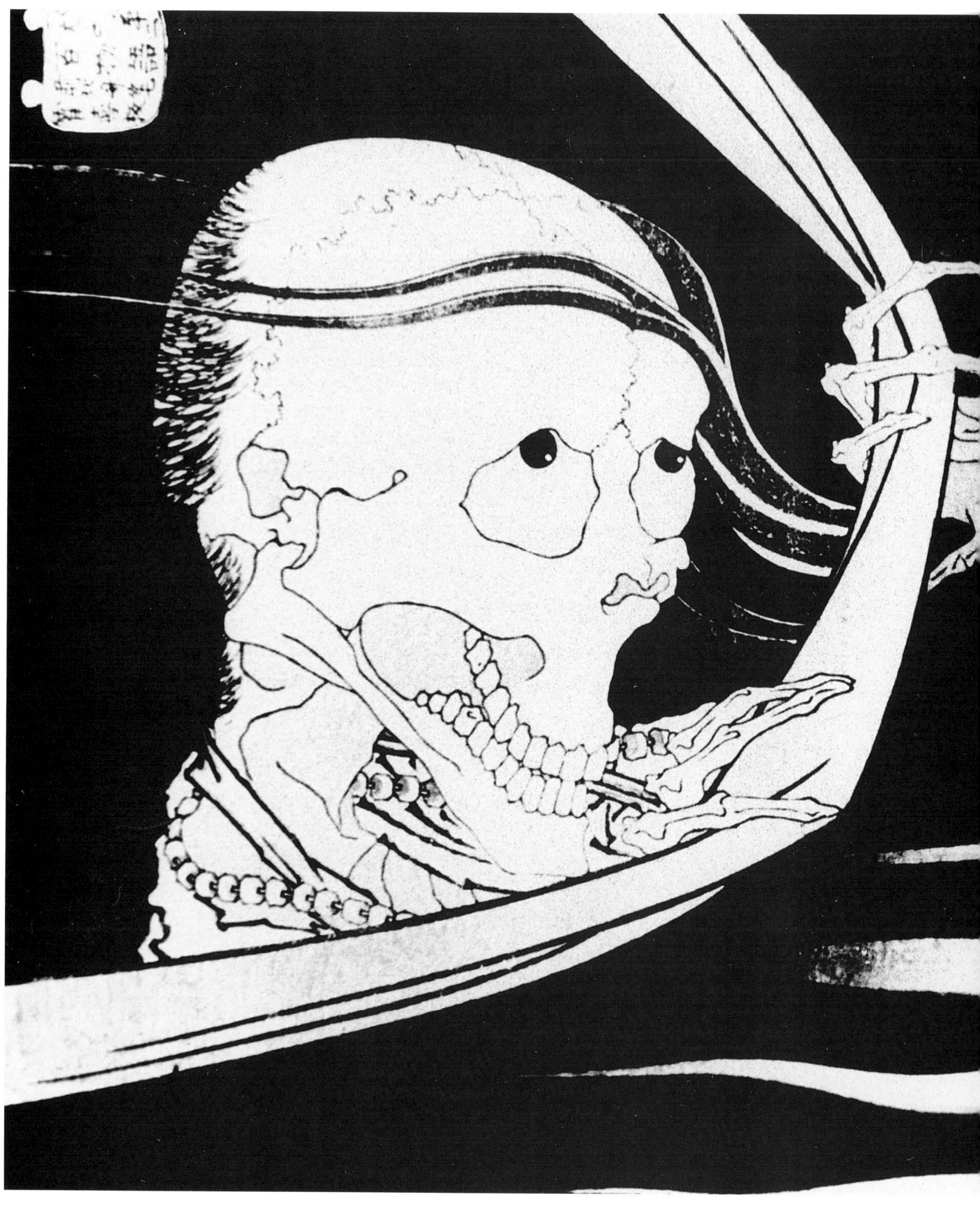

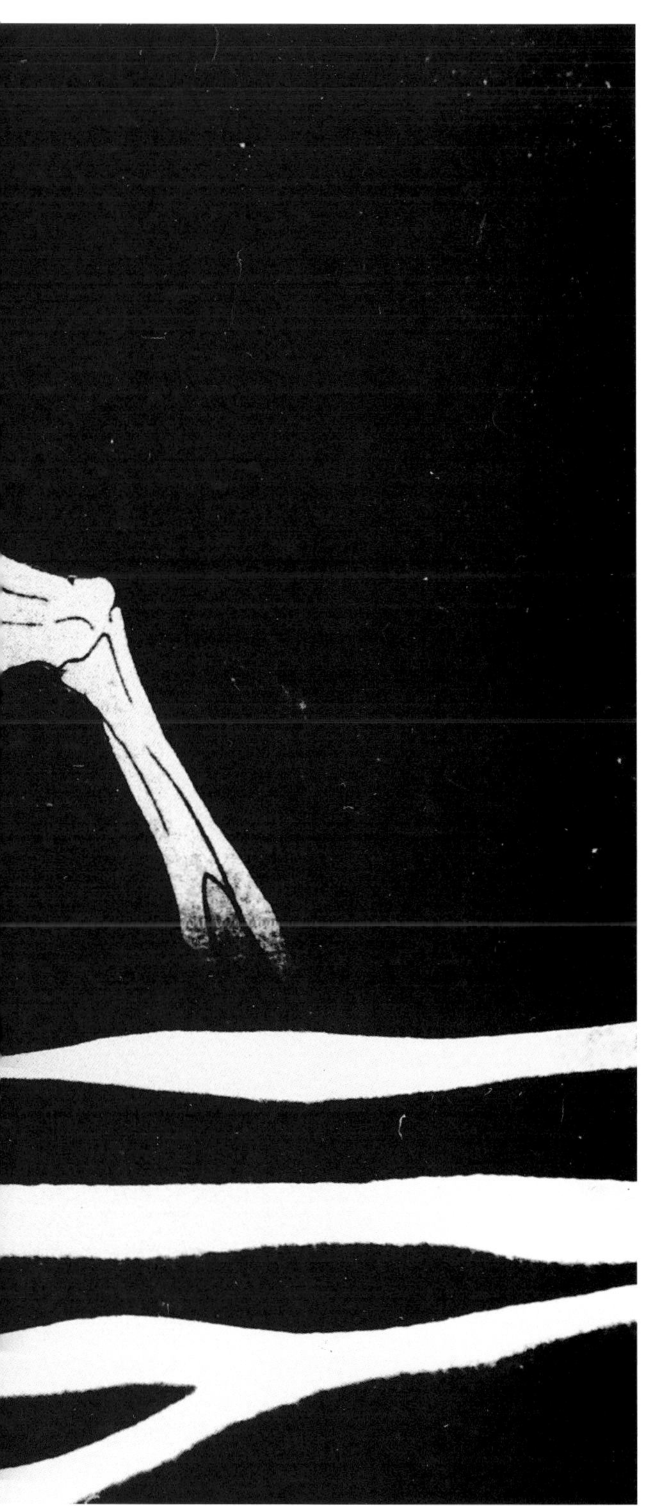

A ghost of Kohada Koheiji from a woodcut after a drawing by the artist Hokusai. Japanese ghosts differ from most others in the maliciousness with which they attack their victims.

punished, and the loss would be forgotten, if only she would become his mistress. However, Okiku still refused him, and in a rage Tessan killed her and cast her body down a well.

From that time on, Okiku's ghost rose up every night from the well: she counted aloud from one to nine, and then vanished. Tessan, racked with guilt, consulted a neighbour, who hid by the well the following night. Okiku's ghost duly arose, and began her slow counting. As she reached 'nine' the neighbour quickly shouted 'Ten!' – and the ghost disappeared, never to return.

In 1803, Santo Kyoden published *A Weird Story of Revenge in the Swamp of Asaka*, a tale that attracted the attention of several writers of *kabuki* plays. This story tells of a certain Kohada Koheiji, who had a faithless wife. Her lover murdered Koheiji and married the widow, but thereafter the couple were haunted constantly by the vengeful ghost of the husband, who eventually drove them both to a violent death.

Another popular *kabuki* theme is that of the princess Takiyasha. She was the daughter of a nobleman who was killed in 940, after rebelling against his overlord. She became a nun after her father's death, but later she and her stepbrother decided to employ sorcery in plotting a second rebellion. They shut themselves up in their father's palace, and began raising fearsome ghosts to assist them in their plans.

However, one of the overlord's warriors, Mitsukui, learnt of the plot, sacked the palace, and despatched not only Takiyasha and her stepbrother, but the supernatural army that they had conjured up.

CHAPTER 6

APPARITIONS AND WRAITHS

Apparitions can coincide with a severe crisis in the lives of the people concerned, but they have also been said to appear up to 12 hours after the moment that that person died.

THE WIFE OF JOHN DONNE

Place: Paris, France

Time: Early 17th century

Reporter: Isaak Walton

Around 1605, the English poet John Donne was obliged to accompany his patron Sir Robert Dudley on a diplomatic trip to Paris. Donne's young wife Anne protested that she was expecting a child and that she could not bear for her husband to be away from her at such a critical time. She said, in fact, that she was very apprehensive that some ill fortune would befall her. Despite all protests, 'Sir Robert became restless in his persuasions for it', and Donne, remembering all the kindnesses that he had received at his patron's hands, found it impossible to refuse.'

The photographer said that there was definitely no one in the church of Eastry in Kent, England, in 1956, when he took this photograph. But the ghostly figure of a clergyman is clearly visible.

It was a 12-day journey to Paris: allowing for a reasonable stay there, Donne did not expect to return until two months were up. A fortnight after he had taken leave of his wife, Sir Robert found Donne pacing up and down in a room of their Paris lodging, 'in such an extacy, and so altered as to his looks, as amazed Sir Robert to behold him.' Donne had been alone less than half an hour, and at first found it impossible to tell Sir Robert what had occurred in such a short time to make him so agitated.

'But after a long and perplexed pause, [he] said "I have seen a dreadful vision since I saw you: I have seen my dear wife pass twice by me through this room, with her hair hanging about her shoulders, and a dead child in her arms..."' Sir Robert replied that he must have fallen asleep, and dreamt what occurred. 'To which Mr Donne's reply was, "I cannot be surer that I now live, than that I have not slept since I saw you, and am sure that at her second appearing, she stopt and lookt at me in the face and vanished."'

The next day, Donne was as confident as ever that he had seen the apparition, and persuaded Sir Robert

DEREK STAFFORD

Derek Stafford was photographing gravestones in the churchyard of St Mary's, Prestbury, not far from Cheltenham in Gloucestershire, on 22 November 1990. He saw no figure in a hooded black cloak, but the ghost of a 'Black Abbot' is reputed to haunt the church and the nearby priory.

LEFT English poet John Donne saw the figure of his wife Anne in his room in Paris when Mrs Donne was suffering a difficult and long childbirth in London, and the baby was stillborn.

to send one of his servants post-haste to England to enquire after Mrs Donne's health. 'The twelfth day the messenger returned with this account – that he found and left Mrs Donne very sad, sick in her bed, and that, after a long and dangerous labour, she had been delivered of a dead child: and upon examination, the abortion proved to be the same day, and about the very hour, that Mr Donne affirmed he saw her pass by him in his chamber.'

COMMENTARY:

In 1601, aged 29, Donne had married Anne More – the 16-year-old niece of Donne's then employer, Sir Thomas Egerton, the Lord Keeper of the Seal –

without her father's consent, and had been briefly imprisoned for it. In the light of this event, and the power of the love poetry that he wrote, we can take it for granted that a strong emotional bond existed between him and his wife.

The physical and spiritual distress that Anne Donne had suffered during her labour, and the intense shock of discovering that the child was stillborn, was sufficient to communicate this 'crisis apparition' to the father. But opinions differ as to whether such an appearance is a ghostly projection or a telepathic perception.

AN AIRMAN RETURNS

Place: Calcutta, India, and England

Time: 19 March, and December, 1917

Reporter: Hubert Wales

Early in the morning of 19 March 1917, Eldred Bowyer-Bower, a British airman with the Royal Flying Corps, was shot down over France and killed. Within 12 hours of his death, he appeared to his half-sister, Mrs Dorothy Spearman, in a Calcutta hotel. As she recalled to Hubert Wales, who collected accounts of the apparition for the Society for Psychical Research: 'At the time I was either sewing or talking to my baby'. As she reported, his appearance – with his 'dear, mischievous look' – was so real that at first she thought he was present in the flesh. She turned to put down her baby safely, and turned back, holding out her hand in greeting. But her brother was no longer there.

'I thought he was only joking,' she later said, 'so I called him and looked everywhere I could think of looking. It was only when I could not find him I became very frightened and the awful fear that he might be dead. I felt very sick and giddy. I think it was two o'clock the baby was christened, and in the church I felt he was there, but I could not see him.'

Around the same time, in England, and long before any notification of Bowyer-Bower's death had been received, the three-year-old daughter of his sister, Mrs Cecily Chater, came into her mother's room and said: 'Uncle Alley-Boy is downstairs.' Mrs Chater reminded her that her uncle (known by this nickname) was in France, but the child persisted. Later that day, Mrs Chater wrote a letter to her mother in which she mentioned the incident – not as anything remarkable, but as evidence that the little girl often thought of her uncle.

In December, some nine months later, the airman's former fiancée woke up to find him sitting beside her on her bed. She spoke to him: 'His lips started to move', and he replied 'just above a whisper'. She reached out her hand, but it passed right through the apparition – and then it vanished.

Also during the month of December, Bowyer-Bower's mother was in bed when she 'came over first very hot and then very cold'. A yellowish-blue ray shone across the room, and moved until it was in front of her. And then: 'Something like a crumpled filmy piece of chiffon unfolded, and the beautiful, wavy top of Eldred's head appeared. A few seconds, and his forehead and broad beautiful brow appeared, still it waited and his lovely blue eyes came, but no mischievous twinkle, but a great intensity. It all shook and quivered, then his tiny little moustache and mouth. I put out my hand and said, "Eldred, I see you", and it all flickered quite out, light and all.'

COMMENTARY:

As G. N. M. Tyrrell says in his book *Apparitions* (1953): 'Of course the child's evidence can be dismissed and the appearance after the death was known assumed to have been subjective hallucinations; but this seems rather thin, for the experience of the airman's mother bears all the marks of a telepathic experience.'

A FLYING ACCIDENT

Place: Scampton RAF Station, Lincolnshire, England

Time: 7 December 1918

Reporter: Lieutenant J. J. Larkin

Shortly before midday on the morning of 7 December 1918, Lieutenant David M'Connel of the RAF, formerly of the Royal Naval Air Service, was asked by his commanding officer to deliver a single-seater Avro 'Camel' biplane from Scampton to Tadcaster, a distance of about 95 km (60 miles). M'Connel looked in on his roommate, Lieutenant Larkin, before he left, saying: 'I expect to get back in time for tea. Cheerio.'

M'Connel was accompanied by another flyer in a two-seater, the intention being that he should be brought back from Tadcaster in this aircraft. As they approached Doncaster, however, both ran into fog, and landed at the airfield there. M'Connel telephoned his flight commander to ask for instructions, and was told: 'Use your own discretion'. He and his companion decided to carry on, but the fog became ever thicker, and the other pilot decided to make an emergency landing.

After circling to make sure that the other pilot was safe, M'Connel flew on towards Tadcaster. Shortly before 3.30 p.m., a girl near the airfield saw the plane side-slip, right itself, and then stall and dive into the ground. She ran to the plane and found M'Connel dead, his head having smashed into the gun in front of him. His watch had stopped on impact: it read 3.25 p.m.

At that time Lieutenant Larkin, M'Connel's roommate, was in his room, reading. 'I was sitting in front of the fire,' he recalled, 'the door of the room being about eight feet [two metres] away at my back. I heard someone walking up the passage; the door opened with the usual noise and clatter that David always made. I heard his "Hello, boy!" and I turned half round in my chair and saw him standing in the doorway, half in and half out of the room, holding the doorknob in his hand.

'He was dressed in his full flying clothes, but wearing his naval cap, there being nothing unusual in his appearance. His cap was pushed back on his head and he was smiling, as he always was when he came into the rooms and greeted us.

'In reply to his "Hello, boy!" I remarked, "Hello, back already?" He replied: "Yes, got there all right, had a good trip"... I was looking at him the whole time he was speaking. He said, "Well, cheerio!" closed the door noisily and went out... I did not have a watch, so cannot be sure of the time, but was certain it was between a quarter and half-past three, because shortly afterwards Lieutenant. Garner-Smith came into the room and it was a quarter to four.'

Garner-Smith remarked that he hoped 'Mac' would be back soon, as they were to go into Lincoln. Larkin replied that he had returned, and was presumably changing. It was later that evening, in the Albion Hotel, Lincoln, that Larkin learnt of M'Connel's crash and death at Tadcaster.

COMMENTARY:

Lieutenant Garner-Smith corroborated Larkin's statement that he had seen and spoken with M'Connel shortly before 3.45 p.m., at a time long before the news of the crash had reached Scampton. Was it a matter of mistaken identity? Larkin wrote: 'The room was quite small, about 12 feet [four metres] square, and at the time the electric light was on… the light was particularly good and bright, and there were no shadows or half-shadows in the room.'

Importantly, only two other men on the station wore naval caps, neither of whom, M'Connel's father insisted, 'could either in height, or build, or manner, or voice, have been mistaken for my son'.

David M'Connel had found his flying helmet quite uncomfortable, and always carried his naval cap in the cockpit with him to change into as soon as possible when he landed, but he was wearing his helmet when he died. It is probable that Lieutenant Larkin, while undoubtedly experiencing the apparition, imagined what he would have expected in normal circumstances: that M'Connel was wearing his cap, and that he reported having had a 'good trip'.

THE OLD MAN OF THE LAKE

Place: Killegar, County Leitrim, Ireland

Time: February 1926

Reporters: Anna Godley and Robert Gallagher, her steward

One afternoon, Miss Anna Godley, who occupied an estate at Killegar in County Leitrim in Ireland, paid a visit to one of her farm labourers, Robert Bowes, who had been ill for some time. Miss Godley had recently broken her leg, and therefore rode in a donkey trap, her steward Robert Gallagher leading the animal, and her masseuse, a Miss Goldsmith, walking behind. They spoke to Bowes

It was across a lake like this that Anna Godley saw Robert Bowes – apparently poling his boat, although no boat was visible – at the exact moment he died in his nearby cottage.

through his cottage window: he sat up in bed and spoke quite strongly, but asked Miss Godley to request that the local doctor come to visit him, as he had not seen him for some time. The party turned for home, taking a road that ran along the shore of a big lake:

'While the steward stopped to open a gate there,' Miss Godley later recalled, 'he asked me "if I saw a man on the lake". I looked and saw an old man with a long white beard which floated in the wind, crossing to the other side of the lake. He appeared to be moving his arms, as though working a punt, but I saw no boat. I said, "Where is the boat?" The steward replied, "There is no boat."

'I said, "What nonsense! there must be a boat, and he is standing up in it", but there was no boat and he was just gliding along on the dark water. The masseuse also saw him. The steward asked me who I thought he was like, I said, "He is exactly like Robert Bowes, the old man". The figure crossed the lake and disappeared among the reeds and trees at the far side, and we came home.'

Miss Godley at once sat down to write a note to be taken to the doctor, but, before she had finished writing, the doctor himself arrived. He had just come from visiting Robert Bowes – taking his car by another road to the cottage – and told her that the old man had passed away only minutes before his arrival.

COMMENTARY:

This is a clear example of a 'crisis apparition'. 'Did Robert as he left this world,' asked Miss Godley, 'cross to take a last look at his old haunts, where he had worked all his life?' This account is also reminiscent of Greek mythology where a dead soul crosses the River Lethe in Charon's boat on its way to the Underworld.

A PHANTASMIC DOUBLE

Place: Near Laramie, Wyoming, USA

Time: Spring 1947

Reporter: Gordon Barrows

Gordon Barrows, later petroleum industry adviser to the United Nations and the World Bank, was discharged from the army and entered the University of Wyoming at Laramie in autumn 1946. In the spring of 1947, he returned to his home to pick up a jeep that he had bought earlier in a sale of surplus army equipment, and then set out to head for Laramie.

Barrows drove for 18 hours. It was now deep into the night and bitterly cold when a blizzard struck. The snow was so thick that cars were stopped and advised to go no further, but Barrows decided to press on. He had just topped a rise, and found the road entering a deep canyon ahead, when he saw a man walking along the road in front.

As the figure was illuminated by the jeep's headlights, Barrows noticed that the man was not unlike himself, and was wearing a Tank Corps jacket like the one he had recently worn in the army. 'Somehow,' he later recounted, 'this odd coincidence seemed the most natural thing in the world.' As the jeep reached the man, he said to Barrows: 'You look exhausted. Want me to drive?'

Barrows willingly surrendered the wheel, and within a few minutes was asleep. The next thing he remembered was coming awake, to find the engine switched off and the man sitting motionless at the wheel. They had emerged from the hills, and Laramie lay just 64 km (40 miles) ahead, on a level road. His passenger refused a lift any further, and climbed out of the jeep. To Barrows' thanks he merely replied, 'You're welcome', and walked off back into the canyon. As Barrows remembered, it all seemed 'like a

LADY PALMER

A photograph taken by Lady Palmer in 1925 in the basilica of Le Bois-Chenu, dedicated to the memory of Joan of Arc, near Domrémy in France. Her friend, Miss Townsend, is the figure in the centre in the hat, but the two figures to the left in white were not in the church at the time.

dream, in which preposterous things seem normal'. But Barrows was convinced that no living being could have survived for long in the cold and snow of the canyon.

COMMENTARY:

Looking back on his experience, Barrows came to the conclusion that his life had been saved by his own double. This is a rare form of apparition, and one that cannot be explained as the result of telepathic projection, but it is not unique. A similar case was reported in Holland in 1944.

A repairman had been asked to correct an adding machine that was malfunctioning at a factory. It was of a make with which he was unfamiliar, and he found that he could not get it to add correctly in hundreds. Then, one night, he awoke in bed to see the machine on his bedside table, illuminated by a bright light. And, leaning over it, he saw himself, fully dressed. He watched as the figure took out a small triangular piece with a pair of pliers, and then replaced it. Next morning he returned to the factory, copied what he had seen the night before – and the machine functioned perfectly.

This second case can be explained away as no more than a dream, the outcome of the brain's ability to continue puzzling away at a problem, and coming up with the correct solution, during sleep. Barrows's experience is less easily dismissed. A possible explanation for both these cases – and others – lies in the theory that time is not a progressive dimension, but that all time co-exists in an infinite series of parallel universes. Sometimes we perceive, in some way, events as they occur within other timeframes.

'Want me to drive?' said the man standing on the side of the road in the middle of nowhere on a snowy night. Gordon Barrows now believes that this stranger who drove him to safety was an apparition of his double.

Laramie
NEXT 4 EXITS

CHAPTER 7

ANIMALS & NON-LIVING APPARITIONS

If we believe that ghosts are a spiritual part of humans that cannot rest after they have died, what can we make of apparitions of animals or even of inanimate objects such as houses, ships and aircraft?

BLACK DOGS

The malevolent phantom of a black dog is commonly believed to be a phenomenon peculiar to the British Isles, but it has also been perceived occasionally in other countries. In fact, the earliest known report comes from France in 856 AD. About halfway through mass, the interior of a small village church was suddenly cast into darkness. The congregation were startled by a large black dog, its eyes blazing fiercely, that had mysteriously appeared, although the church doors were closed. It ran to and fro, and around the altar, as though searching for someone, and then as suddenly disappeared.

A straunge. and terrible Wunder wrought very late in the parish Church of Bongay, a Tovvn of no great distance from the citie of Norwich, namely the fourth of this August, in ye yeere of our Lord 1577. in a great tempest of violent raine, lightning, and thunder, the like wherof hath been seldome seene. With the appearance of an horrible shaped thing, sensibly perceived of the people then and there assembled. Drawen into a plain method according to the written copye. by Abraham Fleming.

LEFT It is old churchyards, like this one, that black dogs are supposed to haunt; a black dog was sometimes buried on the north side of a new cemetery to protect it from the Devil.

RIGHT A pamphlet reporting the 'wunder' of the terrible black dog that appeared in Bungay parish church in Suffolk in 1577.

In Britain, it is popularly believed that the black dog is a harbinger of death, either to the person who sees it, or to a near relative. It is frequently seen in churchyards, or even in a church itself. In Lancashire the phantom is known as Trash or Striker; in East Anglia, Black Shuck; and on the Isle of Man, Moddey Dhoo. The churchyards of both Algarkirk and Northorpe in Lincolnshire also have their resident black dogs. It was once common practice to bury an ordinary black dog on the north side of a new churchyard, in the belief that its spirit would guard the place against visits from the Devil.

Another early report is of a phantom visitation at the church of Blythburgh, in Suffolk, one Sunday morning in 1577. In the middle of the service, a black dog appeared in the aisle, attacked and killed three people, and severely burnt another. It then left, leaving burn marks around the doorway – marks that can still be seen. Soon after, on 4 August, it reappeared in nearby Bungay. A contemporary

In a Yorkshire story, a white sheepdog guards the place where his master was murdered. Like many dog sightings, it is seen on a bridge across a waterway.

pamphlet describes the 'straunge and terrible Wunder wroughte very late in the parish Church of Bongay'; the extreme weather conditions when it appeared 'in a great tempest of violent raine, lightning and thunder'; and its unusual appearance, 'the like whereof hath been seldome seene… an horrible shaped thing, sensibly perceived of the people then and there assembled'. The accompanying woodcut shows an image of a large black dog.

Was it this same dog that was seen nearly four centuries later, on a fine summer evening in 1938, on the Suffolk–Norfolk border, just a few miles from Bungay? A man out for an evening stroll, in a lane bordered by steep banks on both sides, noticed a large black dog coming towards him. It had materialized and, as it was a fierce-looking creature, he stepped aside to let it pass. But, after it had drawn level with him, it vanished. He reported that the dog was unusually large, with a very shaggy coat, and that its eyes were fiery red.

Sites such as this – old trackways and green lanes – also seem to be favoured by the phantom dogs. On a green lane at Uplyme in Devon there is an inn called, significantly, The Black Dog. Devon, in fact, has many black dogs. One has often been seen on an ancient track between Copplestone and Great Torrington; Okehampton Castle has its Black Hound; and another is reported at Hayne Manor in Stowford, not far away.

Many other prehistoric sites have their guardian black dogs: one is seen standing guard at Doghill Barrow, near Stonehenge in Wiltshire, and several have been reported at Sixhills, near Stevenage in Hertfordshire. In Wales, at the Devil's Nags, on Cot Moor in Pembrokeshire, and at a stone circle near Amlwch, on Anglesey, apparitions of guardian dogs are regularly reported.

In Scotland, the resonant names of Caisteal a Choin Dubh (Black Dog Castle), near Craignish, and Dun a Choin Dubh (Black Dog Fort), at Knapdale, tell their own story.

A strange tale is told by writer Augustus Hare in his autobiography *In My Solitary Life*. In the mid-19th century, the owners of Blickling Hall in Norfolk, Lord and Lady Lothian, decided to have some partition walls taken down. An old woman in the village told the local clergyman that this would cause trouble:

BAYARD, THE PHANTOM HORSE

Phantom horses are rarely encountered without riders. One of the most famous is Bayard, the wonder horse of Renaud, who was one of the four renowned sons of Aymon and a paladin of Emperor Charlemagne in the 8th century. Renaud was eventually declared an outlaw and was besieged in the castle of Montauban, France, for seven years. When he finally made peace, he was sent on a pilgrimage to Jerusalem, and Bayard was thrown into the River Meuse with a millstone round his neck. But the horse escaped, and his ghost can still be seen in the Ardennes. Where houses have been built over his old haunts, Bayard may even appear at night to terrify some unsuspecting sleeper.

'... because of the dog. Don't you know that when A. was fishing in the lake he caught an enormous fish, and that, when it was landed, a great black dog came out of its mouth? They never could get rid of that dog, who kept going round and round in circles inside the house, till they sent for a wise man from London, who opposed the straight lines of the partitions to the lines of the circles, and so quieted the dog. But if these young people pull down the partitions, they will let the dog loose again, and there's not a wise man in all London could lay that dog now.'

The black dog is still with us. During a winter night in 1972, at an isolated farmhouse on the south side of Dartmoor, a farmer and his wife were awakened by scratching noises at their bedroom door. The farmer took up a poker, and opened the door: 'Then suddenly I could see a large shadow at the top of the stairs. For some reason I assumed it was a dog, and was about to turf it out of the house, when it suddenly moved toward me, its eyes glowing a fiery red. I was so shocked, I don't really know why, that I just struck out at it.'

As he swung the poker at the dark creature, there was a brilliant flash of light, followed by the sound of breaking glass, and the dog vanished. The farmer and his wife searched the house: they found that the electricity had failed completely, every window was broken, and the yard was covered with broken tiles from the roof. In the morning, they found that the roofs of the barns and outhouses had also been severely damaged.

Others who had struck out at black dogs suffered even worse. In 1893, two men driving a cart along a Norfolk lane were forced to rein up at the sudden appearance of a black dog in their path. Although his passenger, sure that this was Black Shuck, begged him not to, the driver whipped up his horse and drove straight at the phantom. As the cart touched it, the dog, its eyes flaming with rage, disappeared in a ball of fire. Within days, the driver was dead.

In 1927, a friend of Walter Gill, a Manx writer, encountered a black dog on a road near Ramsey on the Isle of Man. The phantom refused to let him pass, staring at him with eyes 'as burning coals'. Eventually the dog moved aside, but within a few days that man's father had died.

COMMENTARY:

It would be easy to dismiss these stories as having a perfectly natural explanation: large fierce dogs are a common sight in the countryside, and they can easily squeeze through relatively small openings to appear and disappear at will. However, in numerous cases, the regularity of sightings over many years can only be accounted for by assuming that generation after generation of dogs has patrolled the same site. A significant factor in certain appearances has been the occurrence of a sudden violent electric storm, a phenomenon also associated with other kinds of paranormal events.

Another factor to be taken into consideration is the association of the black dogs with prehistoric sites – not only ancient trackways and burial mounds, but long-established churches, which were frequently built over 'pagan' places of worship. We have seen how malign presences can be connected with ancient burial sites, and some writers have suggested that the black dogs are the ghosts of animals that – thousands of years ago – were set to guard sacred sites.

A connection with old watercourses has also been suggested. In Suffolk, a black dog is often reported standing by the edge of a boundary stream; in Somerset, the dog that haunts one stretch of road near Butleigh Hill always vanishes as it reaches a particular bridge; the same phenomenon has been observed at a bridge that crosses two loughs at Pontoon, County Mayo, in Ireland.

The theory was investigated by Ivan Bunn, who undertook research into the Black Shuck of East

Anglia. He noted that, out of 62 reported sightings, 15 were very near a main river, and 31 were on or near the seacoast. In their book *Alien Animals* (1980), Janet and Colin Bord, who collected more than 150 reports of black dog sightings, suggested that there is an association, not only with open water, but with underground watercourses. Leys, the mysterious cross-country lines that link a succession of ancient sites, also appear to have some connection.

The many black dogs of Devon, particularly on or around Dartmoor, found an interesting echo during the mid-1990s. The Ministry of Agriculture was compelled to mount an inquiry into numerous reports of a 'black puma' that ranged the moor and savaged the sheep grazing there. Farmers were convinced that the animal was larger and fiercer than any ordinary dog, and there were numerous sightings. The Ministry published their report in 1995, insisting that there was no evidence of any such beast being at large, although local people insisted on what they had seen. Could it have been the phantom dog, with its fiercely blazing eyes, that had been a part of Dartmoor legend for centuries?

IN THE TOWER OF LONDON

Place: The Tower, London

Time: October 1817

Reporter: Edmund Lenthal Swifte

The Tower of London, with its centuries of murders and executions, is popularly believed to be haunted by a host of ghosts, not least that of Henry VIII's second wife, Anne Boleyn, whom he had had beheaded

In 1817, one of the Jewel House sentries was alarmed by a figure 'like a huge bear'. He attacked with his bayonet, but collapsed in a fit and died within days.

Jewel
House

SOUTH-EAST VIEW OF THE JEWEL TOWER.

The Old Jewel House of the Tower of London. It was here that the Keeper of the Jewels, Edmund Swifte, observed 'a cylindrical figure... hovering between the ceiling and the table'.

and whose ghost appears 'with her head tucked underneath her arm'.

But one of the most unusual apparitions was seen by Edmund Swifte, the Keeper of the Crown Jewels, and reported by him in *Notes & Queries* in 1860: 'One Saturday night in October 1817, about the witching hour, I was at supper with my wife, her sister, and our little boy, in the sitting room of the Jewel House… The doors were all closed, heavy and dark cloth curtains were let down over the windows, and the only light in the room was that of two candles on the table… I had offered a glass of wine to my wife when, on putting it to her lips, she paused and exclaimed, "Good God! What is that?" I looked up, and saw a cylindrical figure, like a glass-tube, seemingly about the thickness of my arm, and hovering between the ceiling and the table; its contents appeared to be a dense fluid, white and pale azure, like to the gathering of a summer-cloud, and incessantly mingling within the cylinder. This lasted about two minutes, when it began to move slowly before my sister-in-law; then, following the oblong shape of the table, before my son and myself; passing behind my wife, it paused for a moment over her right shoulder (observe, there was no mirror opposite to her in which she could there behold it).

'Instantly she crouched down, and with both hands covering her shoulder, she shrieked out, "O Christ! It has seized me!" Even now, while writing, I feel the fresh horror of that moment. I caught up my chair, struck at the wainscot behind her, rushed upstairs to the other children's room, and told the terrified nurse what I had seen… The marvel of all this is enhanced by the fact that neither my sister-in-law nor my son beheld this "appearance".'

After morning service, Swifte told the chaplain of his experience. He wondered whether there might not be a simple explanation, and 'proposed the visit of a scientific friend, who minutely inspected the parlour, and made the closest investigation, but could not in any way solve the mystery'.

COMMENTARY:

Were it not for the fact that two of the four persons in the room did not see the apparition, it might be dismissed as the occurrence of that mysterious and still unexplained phenomenon: ball lightning. The suggestion that somebody, in another building in the Tower, had been playing with light reflected from a mirror does not stand up to Swifte's insistence that all the curtains were closely drawn.

The Keeper reported another incident of a similar nature that took place shortly afterwards. One of the night sentries at the Jewel House was alarmed by a figure 'like a huge bear', coming from beneath the door to the jewel room. 'He thrust at it with his bayonet, which stuck in the door, even as my chair dinted the wainscot; he dropped in a fit, and was carried to the guardroom.'

The sentry's companion testified that he had been awake and alert, and Swifte heard the story from the man's own lips. But 'in another day or two the brave and steady soldier, who would have mounted a breach or led a forlorn hope with unshaken nerves, died at the presence of a shadow'.

Whether this was another form of the same phenomenon witnessed by Swifte, we do not know. Observers of the paranormal sometimes project their own expectations upon what they observe: Swifte was at dinner in his own home, and knew that no light could intrude from outside; the soldier, on the other hand, very probably knew that for three centuries the Tower had housed the royal menagerie, which included a number of bears.

THE FLYING DUTCHMAN?

Place: Off the Cape of Good Hope, Africa

Time: 27 January 1923

Observer: 4th Officer N. K. Stone

It was on 26 January 1923 that the P & O liner SS *Barrabool* left Cape Town bound for London. At midnight, two officers, the quartermaster and a cadet took over the watch on the vessel's bridge. Shortly after, wrote the 2nd officer, 'I distinctly saw the silvery appearance of a full-rigged sailing ship… No sails were set, or in other words, the yards were bare. The only conclusion was that the vessel was a derelict, and abandoned, when to our increasing amazement she simply vanished.' As the 4th officer, Mr Stone, reported the incident:

'About 0.15 a.m. we noticed a strange "light" on the port bow; I may add here that it was a very dark night, overcast, with no moon. We looked at this through binoculars and the ship's telescope, and made out what appeared to be the hull of a sailing ship, luminous, with two distinct masts carrying bare yards, also luminous: no sails were visible, but there was a luminous haze between the masts. There were no navigation lights, and she appeared to be coming closer to us and at about the same speed as ourselves. When first sighted she was about two to three miles [four to five km] away, and when within about a half a mile [800 metres] of us she suddenly disappeared. 'There were four witnesses of this spectacle, the 2nd officer, a cadet, the helmsman and myself. I shall never forget the 2nd officer's startled expression – "My God, Stone, it's a ghost ship".'

Stone subsequently drew a sketch of the ship, and 'many people who have seen it wonder if she was the *Flying Dutchman* we saw that night'.

An earlier sighting of the ghost ship is found in *The Cruise of Her Majesty's Ship Baccante*, a record of a naval voyage taken in 1881 by George, Prince of Wales (later King George V), and his elder brother the Duke of Clarence. An entry in the princes' journal for one night aboard HMS *Inconstant* reads:

'June 11th, 1881: At 4 a.m. the *Flying Dutchman* crossed our bows. A strange red light as of a phantom ship all aglow in the midst of which light the masts, spars of a brig 200 yards [180 metres]

COACH OF BONES

This 'coach of bones' was cleverly animated by the early filmmaker Georges Méliès for *The Merry Frolics of Satan*, but the story of such a coach is also told at Okehampton on Dartmoor. In it rides the wicked Lady Howard, and the coach is made of the bones of her four husbands, all of whom she murdered. In front of it runs her skeletal hound, which must fetch a blade of grass from Okehampton Park each night, until every blade has been plucked – when the world will come to an end.

distant stood out in strong relief… The lookout man on the forecastle reported her as close on the port bow, where also the officer of the watch from the bridge clearly saw her, as did also the quarterdeck midshipman, who was sent forward to the forecastle, but found no vestige or sign whatsoever of the ship was seen either near or right away on the horizon, the night being clear, the sea calm.

'Thirteen persons altogether saw her, but whether it was… the *Flying Dutchman* or what else must remain unknown. The *Tourmaline* and *Cleopatra*, who were sailing on our starboard bow, flashed to ask whether we had seen the strange red light.'

Some 13 people aboard the *Inconstant* saw the phantom ship, together with more witnesses aboard the accompanying vessels.

The fearsome ghost ship *Flying Dutchman* haunts the seas off the Cape of Good Hope. Its skipper, perhaps the daring Bernard Fokke, is doomed to sail the seas for eternity after entering into a pact with the Devil.

COMMENTARY:

The legend of the *Flying Dutchman* was, of course, well known to these sailors. The story begins with a certain Bernard Fokke, famous as a daring mariner in the 17th century. It is said that he strengthened the masts of his ship with iron, and made notoriously rapid passages to the East Indies as a result. Because of this, he was rumoured to have made a pact with the Devil, and, when he and his ship later disappeared without trace, substance was added to the tale.

A small squadron of Royal Navy ships, including the brig HMS *Barracouta*, was despatched in 1821 to explore and survey the coasts of Arabia and Africa. Captain Owen, commanding HMS *Severn*, reported that the squadron was scattered by adverse winds off the Cape of Good Hope:

'In the evening of April 6th, when off Port Danger, the *Barracouta* was seen about two miles [three km] to leeward. Struck with the singularity of her being so soon after us, we at first concluded that it could not be she; but the peculiarity of her rigging and other circumstances convinced us that we were mistaken… After keeping thus for some time, we became surprised that she made no effort to join us, but on the contrary stood away… During the night we could not perceive any light or indication of her locality. The next morning we anchored in Simon's Bay, where for a whole week we were in anxious expectation of her arrival; but it afterwards appeared that at this period the *Barracouta* must have been above 300 miles [480km] from us, and no other vessel of the same class was ever seen about the Cape.'

This may well have been the source of an anonymous tale published in *Blackwood's Magazine* in the same year, and was the theme of a melodrama entitled *The Flying Dutchman* that was popular a few years later. The story was embroidered by Auguste Jal in his book *Scènes de la Vie Maritime* (Scenes from Life at Sea, 1832), adopted by the poet Heinrich Heine in 1834, and subsequently became the subject of a novel by Captain Marryat, *The Phantom Ship* (1839). It was from these sources that Wagner developed the scenario for his opera *Der Fliegende Holländer* in 1843.

It must be remembered that, in 1923, there were still many sailing ships on the run between Australia and Europe. Also, a phenomenon familiar to most sailors was 'St Elmo's fire', an electrostatic glow that enveloped the upper masts in certain atmospheric conditions. It is conceivable that what the officers aboard the *Barrabool* saw was a real ship, possibly running without navigation lights, and that her 'disappearance' was due to the dissipation of the electric glow around her masts and sails. But this goes no way to explain the experience of the captain of the *Severn*, nor the persistence of the legend of the 'Flying Dutchman'.

THE CAT OF KILLAKEE

Place: Killakee Art Centre, Dublin Mountains, Ireland

Time: 1968–1970

Reporter: Margaret O'Brien

The Dower House at Killakee, in the mountains not far from Dublin, was almost derelict when Mrs Margaret O'Brien decided to open an art centre there early in 1968. When she and her husband Nicholas moved in: 'a group of workmen from Kilbeggan had been rebuilding the premises and living on the site in the meantime. We discovered that they had been disturbed by odd things happening in the night – strange sounds, locked doors opening by themselves and, worst of all, the appearance of a huge black cat.'

Tom McAssey, a painter working on the house, described how, when he and two others were working one evening, the room suddenly turned icy-cold. Some time before, the door had been closed; now they saw that it was open.

McAssey saw a shadowy shape in the darkness beyond the door. 'At first I thought someone was playing a joke,' he recalled, 'and I said "Come in, I see you." There was a deep sort of guttural growl, and the three of us turned and ran in panic. We slammed the door behind us, and I turned and looked back. The door was open again, and a monstrous black cat with red-flecked amber eyes crouched there in the half-light, I thought my legs wouldn't take me away from the place.'

'I thought the whole thing was nonsense,' Mrs O'Brien said later. 'A group of country people sitting alone in an empty house on a lonely hillside at night, telling each other stories and frightening themselves. Then I saw the creature myself, and I began to understand their fear.'

Mrs O'Brien reported that the animal was 'about the size of an Airedale', squatting on the flagstones of the hall. All the doors of the house were locked before the cat materialized, and they remained locked when it disappeared.

Distressed by the sight of the apparition, by the other disturbances, and by what she had been told, Mrs O'Brien decided to have the house exorcised. For 12 months all seemed quiet, and then, in the autumn of 1969, a lively party of Irish show-business folk who were visiting the art centre decided to hold a seance. 'After this,' said Mrs O'Brien, 'disturbances began again. Paintings were torn apart, crockery smashed… bottles broken, and the sound of ringing bells was heard… '

Early in 1970, Mrs O'Brien saw the figures of two nuns walk through the gallery of the centre. A medium who was brought to the house by RTE Television declared that they were the ghosts of two women who had assisted at blasphemous 'black masses' held by the 18th-century 'Hell Fire Club' on nearby Montpelier Hill. In July, Mrs O'Brien had the house and the grounds exorcised again, and from then on, apart from 'the odd bump in the night', all was quiet.

COMMENTARY:

The haunting seems to have a close connection with local legends concerning the activities of the Hell Fire Club. One story told how the club's riotous members had once tormented a deformed boy for sport, then throttled him and buried his dead body. Beneath the flagstones of the room in which the unfortunate deformed boy was said to have been killed, Mrs O'Brien found a metal statue of a boyish Puck figure attached to a font of white marble. Significantly, during the course of the building operations early in 1968, a grave was uncovered in the garden, containing a small human skeleton with a huge skull. It was around this time that the phantom black cat was first seen.

Many other stories are attached to the Dower House. It is said that poet W. B. Yeats and fellow members of the esoteric Order of the Golden Dawn held their ceremonies there at the turn of the century. Later, the house belonged to Countess Markievicz, one of the foremost members of the Easter Rebellion of 1916. She arranged for it to be a refuge for members of the IRA in the 1920s, and one was shot and killed there.

Unfortunately, none of these local legends suggests an explanation for the black cat. In some ways, it seems, like the black dogs described earlier, to have been the guardian of a grave. The unearthing of the unhappy boy's skeleton might have let loose psychical forces, which could have manifested themselves in a variety of phenomena, and then gradually dissipated.

CHAPTER 8

MISCHIEVOUS SPIRITS

Many have dismissed poltergeists as nothing more than an attempt by a pubescent girl either to seek attention or to work out some kind of revenge. However, there are a number of cases in which the activity appears to be due to an external intelligence.

The word poltergeist is the German for 'noisy sprite', one of those 'things that go bump in the night'. Although the word has only been used in psychical research since the late 19th century, the phenomenon has been recorded for hundreds of years, as several of the following cases show.

Poltergeist manifestations include a remarkable variety of events: the movement of domestic objects, showers of mud or stones, the teleportation of objects into closed and locked rooms, and many different sorts of noises, knocking, banging and scratching, as well as what appear to be imitations of human whistling or speech.

In certain cases, these relatively harmless – if frightening – occurrences escalate into something more serious: fires, stigmata and other forms of physical attack. And researchers have drawn attention to what appears to be a generally consistent factor in all poltergeist manifestations: the central presence of a young person, usually a premenstrual or pubescent girl.

An engraving of a poltergeist attack in a late Victorian household. Pans, tongs and other objects are being hurled at the sleeping child, to the horror of the family and their maidservant.

A VISITATION IN LE MANS

Place: Le Mans, France

Time: 1135

Victims: Provost Nicholas and his wife Amica

One day in 1135, or thereabouts, Provost Nicholas and his neighbours in Le Mans were extremely alarmed by 'uproar and fearful noises, as if a spirit had thrown enormous stones against the walls, with a force that shook the roof, walls, and ceilings'. The disturbances continued: dishes and plates were moved from one place to another by an unseen hand; a candle burst into flame, 'though very far from the fire'; and sometimes, when a meal was placed on the table, bran, ashes or soot were scattered over it, making it inedible. Nicholas's wife

LEGIONS OF HELL

For people in the Middle Ages, poltergeist activity could only be explained as an attack upon the household by vicious demons, described as the 'legions of Hell', as illustrated in this decorated chapter initial from Collin de Plancy's *Dictionnaire Infernal.*

After unexplained noises at the home of the Provost Nicholas in the French town of Le Mans in 1135, priests sprinkled holy water around the house. In many religions, holy water is believed to repel evil.

Amica, who had wound some thread to be woven into cloth, found it 'twisted and ravelled in such a way, that all who saw it could not sufficiently admire the manner in which it was done'.

Priests were sent for, who sprinkled holy water everywhere around the house. On the second night, a voice was heard, 'as it were the voice of a young girl, who, with sighs that seemed drawn from the bottom of her heart, said in a lamentable and sobbing voice, that her name was Garnier; and, addressing herself to the provost, said: "Alas! Whence do I come? From what distant country, through how many storms, dangers, through snow, cold, fire, and bad weather, have I arrived at this place! I have not received power to harm any one – but prepare yourselves with the sign of the cross against a band of evil spirits, who are here only to do you harm; have a mass of the Holy Ghost said for me, and a mass for those defunct; and you, my dear sister-in-law, give some clothes to the poor for me".'

The assembled company asked the entity a number of questions, 'to which it replied very pertinently… but it would not enter into any argument, nor yet into conference with learned men who were sent by the Bishop of Le Mans; this last circumstance is very remarkable, and cast some suspicion on this apparition'.

COMMENTARY:

We owe this account to *Le Monde Fantôme* by Augustin Calmet, written six centuries after the event. We do not know its source, nor whether the typical poltergeist phenomena continued, and the report is right to 'cast some suspicion on this apparition'. More recent experience suggests that, even when a voice is heard, as in the case of the 'Bell Witch' in Tennessee in the early 19th century, it seldom has more than a few words to say, and certainly does not make a long speech like that detailed above. It is possible that a woman in the room – conceivably Nicholas's wife Amica – went into trance, and that what we have is a tidied-up transcript of what she said.

The poltergeist activity may well have been unconnected, particularly as the voice declared that it was there to warn against 'a band of evil spirits'. If so, we have no means of knowing whether an adolescent, the usual focus of such activity, was present. However, although the account does not tell us, it is probable that Provost Nicholas and his wife had children.

THE STOCKWELL POLTERGEIST

Place: Stockwell, south London, England

Time: 6–7 January 1772

Victims and witnesses: Mrs Mary Golding, owner of the house; Ann Robinson, her maid; Mary Pain, her niece; John Pain, Mary's husband; Mary Martin, Mr Pain's servant; Richard Fowler, a neighbour; Sarah Fowler, his wife

At the date of this incident, Stockwell, in the London parish of Lambeth, was still largely open country, with several farms in the vicinity, one of which was John Pain's. At about 10 a.m. on 6 January, Mrs Mary Golding was in her parlour when she heard glass and china falling in her kitchen. Her maid, Ann Robinson, called her, and she went to the kitchen in time to see a row of plates fall by themselves from a shelf. Almost at once, things began to fall and break all over the house: a clock, a pan of salt beef, a lantern on the staircase. The noise, and Mrs Golding's cries, brought several people to the scene. One of these was a carpenter, Mr Rowlidge, who declared that the cause was obvious – the foundations of the house were giving way.

Mrs Golding fled into the house of her nearest neighbour, a Mr Gresham – where she fainted – while Mr Rowlidge and the others began to remove her belongings from the house and carry them into Mr Gresham's. All were amazed at the cool calm of the maid, who did not seem to be at all surprised at what

Stockwell Common in 1792. Ann Robinson, the maid suspected of causing the Stockwell disturbances, later implausibly claimed she had fabricated the events. Was she covering up for her own telekinetic powers?

UNNATURAL FORCES

In this photograph of poltergeist activity at Dodleston, Chester, in May 1985, all the furniture can be seen uplifted and hurled to the far end of the room. Many smaller items were also thrown around.

was happening, and had to be persuaded to follow her mistress. Somebody ran to the Pain's farmhouse to fetch Mrs Golding's niece Mary, telling her that her aunt was dying, and somebody else fetched a surgeon.

Mrs Golding recovered from her faint, and was bled by the surgeon, who left the blood in his bowl, to be examined later. However, the blood had scarcely congealed when it sprang out of the bowl on to the floor, and the bowl broke in pieces. A bottle of rum standing beside it broke at the same time.

Among the things carried out of Mrs Golding's house was a large mirror, which was taken into Mr Gresham's house and laid down below the sideboard: shortly after, all the glass and china on the sideboard fell down on to it and broke it. And when the neighbours were offered a choice of a glass of wine or rum, both bottles broke before they were uncorked.

By now, Mrs Golding was in a frantic state, and was persuaded to go to her niece's home. While they ate a meal together, the maid was sent back to see whether anything further had happened at Mrs Golding's house, and in her absence all was quiet. However, when she returned in the evening, a row of pewter dishes fell from a shelf and then, when they had finished rolling about the floor, suddenly turned upside down. They were put back, and immediately fell again, and then a second row of dishes followed them. An egg that was on the shelf beside them flew across the kitchen, and struck the cat on the head.

A pestle and mortar on the chimney shelf jumped onto the floor; then brass candlesticks and other items. The family decided to put all the china and glass on the floor, but this was to no avail, because the dishes began to dance about and broke in pieces, and a teapot flew across the room and hit the maid's foot. A teacup was carried right across the kitchen, 'ringing like a bell', and smashed to pieces against the dresser.

All the time, the maid Ann was strolling calmly about, and could not be persuaded to sit down. She told her mistress not to be alarmed, saying that events like this could be expected in any family. At about 10 p.m., Richard Fowler was asked to come over from his neighbouring house to observe what was happening, and give some comfort, but he was so terrified that three hours later he refused to stay any longer in the farmhouse.

By 5 a.m. on the following morning Mrs Golding announced that she could stay in the Pains' house no longer and was going to Richard Fowler's: now the tables and chairs were being thrown about, and the scene of destruction was 'amazing beyond all description'. Her maid stayed to help dress the children, who had been put in the barn, for fear the house was falling down, but when they arrived at the Fowler home the phenomena began there. Candlesticks were thrown over, a lantern fell from its hook, and a basket of coal was upset all over the floor. At this, Richard Fowler turned on Mrs Golding and begged her to leave his house, asking her what dreadful crime she had committed to bring such punishment upon herself.

The poor woman drew upon her last reserves of self-possession, and told him that her conscience was clear, and 'she could as well wait the will of providence in her own house as in any other place whatever'. Accompanied by John Pain, she and her maid returned home. But as soon as they arrived there, a cask of beer in the cellar turned upside down, a pail of water 'boiled like a pot', and a table in the parlour was turned over.

Ann Robinson was sent to fetch Mrs Pain, and it seems clear that, while the maid was gone, Mrs Golding and Pain discussed the events. They decided that Ann Robinson must be the cause, because on her return she was immediately dismissed and told to leave the house. From that time onwards, there were no further disturbances.

When all the broken glass and china at Mrs Golding's had been swept up, it filled three large pails and, at Mrs Pain's, two more. A detailed report of these occurrences was published as a pamphlet in London some weeks later.

COMMENTARY:

Ann Robinson was said to have been about 20 years of age, and she had been in Mrs Golding's employment for only 10 days. As with so many other poltergeist cases, a young woman or teenage girl was the focus for the disturbances.

Fifty years later, the case was reviewed in William Hone's *Everyday Book* (1826). A Mr Braidley stated that, many years after the Stockwell incidents, he had had a conversation with Ann Robinson, who claimed that she had produced the phenomena by attaching horse-hairs and wires to the crockery and the other household objects. 'When she saw the effect of her first feats, she was tempted to exercise the dexterity beyond her original purpose for mere amusement,' wrote Hone. 'She was astonished at the astonishment she caused, and so went from one thing to another; and being quick in her motions and shrewd, she puzzled all the simple old people, and nearly frightened them to death.'

It will be obvious, from the description of what took place, that this allegation is, to say the least, implausible. What seems most likely is that Ann, herself puzzled and disturbed by what took place, but aware that she was somehow the cause, gradually persuaded herself that she had produced the phenomena by physical means, rather than accept the existence of some occult force beyond her control.

THE ROCHESTER RAPPINGS

Place: Hydesville, near Rochester, New York, USA

Time: 1847–1848

Victims: John Fox, his wife Margaret, and daughters Margaretta, aged 14 and Kate (Cathie), aged 12

The Fox family moved into a small two-storeyed wooden cottage in Hydesville, a village of New York State, in December 1847. Soon after, they began to hear knocking sounds coming from the walls. Disturbed, but more curious than alarmed, they discovered that they could elicit imitations of the clapping of their hands, and even answers to

Margaretta Fox, whose public demonstrations of poltergeist-type rappings led to the establishment of the Spiritualist movement. She and her sister Kate were later accused of fraud.

questions. As Margaret Fox described the events of 31 March 1848:

'It was very early when we went to bed on this night – hardly dark. I had been so broken of rest I was almost sick – I had just laid down when it commenced as usual – the children, who slept in the other bed in the room, heard the rapping, and tried to make similar sounds by snapping their fingers. My youngest child, Cathie, said: "Mr Splitfoot, do as I do", clapping her hands. The sound instantly followed her with the same number of raps. When she stopped the sound ceased for a short time… I then thought I could put a test that no one in the place could answer. I asked the "noise" to rap my different children's ages successively. Instantly, each one of my children's ages was given correctly, pausing between them sufficiently long enough to individualize them until the seventh – at which a longer pause was made, and then three more emphatic raps were given, corresponding to the age of the little one that died, which was my youngest child. I then asked: "Is this a human being that answers my questions correctly?" There was no rap. I asked: "Is it a spirit? If it is, make two raps." Two sounds were given as soon as the request was made.'

Some of the neighbours were called in to witness the happenings. One was Chauncey Losey, who asked the entity about his personal affairs, and closed his written deposition on his experience with the words: 'I think that no human being could have answered all the questions that were answered by this rapping.'

News of the 'haunting' spread, and crowds of sensation-seekers came to the Fox's home, where John Fox claimed that the rapping entity had revealed that it was the spirit of a travelling salesman

The cottage of the Fox family at Hydesville, New York State. The rappings were heard on the walls and made answers to questions that were allegedly known only to the questioner.

When Kate Fox, above, and Margaretta demonstrated how they communicated with spirits they caused a sensation, though some claimed that the 'rappings from the dead' were created by the girls' knee joints.

who had been murdered in the house some time before. E. E. Lewis, a local publisher who investigated the events, learnt that previous occupants had also been disturbed, and one person even claimed to have heard of the murder, but there was no firm evidence. Later reports suggested that human remains had been found buried in the cellar, but this story was never substantiated.

Mrs Fox took her two daughters to stay with a married daughter in Rochester, and there, in 1849, the girls gave their first public demonstration, following it up with many other performances throughout the eastern United States. They created a sensation, and their fame was unaffected by the suggestion of three distinguished professors from Buffalo that the raps were created by movements of the girls' knee joints, or by the allegation that Kate had confessed to making the sounds simply by cracking her toes.

COMMENTARY:

The particular interest of this case lies in the fact that it brought about the establishment of the Spiritualist movement, in which communicating with the dead through 'spirit rapping' became an essential part. The Fox sisters turned professional mediums, and were the subject of numerous psychical investigations. Some researchers, such as William Crookes, were impressed, while others dismissed them as frauds. Their later careers were marked with tragedy: they suffered mob violence, sank into alcoholism, and at last confessed to fraud – only to retract the confession subsequently.

There is considerable doubt attached even to the earliest events. The two girls slept in the same room as their parents, and Mrs Fox's belief that 'no one in the place' would know the ages of her children is extremely naive. Whether the rappings truly gave answers that could be known only to Chauncey Losey, we do not know. The verdict of most modern writers has been that Margaretta and Kate Fox were guilty of fraud throughout their lives.

SPIRIT IN A BOTTLE

Place: Seaford, Long Island, USA

Time: February 1958

Victims: James and Lucille Herrmann, and their children, Jimmy and Lucille

At about 3.30 p.m. on the afternoon of 3 February 1958, Mrs Lucille Herrmann was startled to hear a succession of popping sounds throughout her house in Seaford, Nassau County, Long Island. Followed by her children, Jimmy, 12, and Lucille, 13, she hurried to find out what had happened, and discovered, in nearly every room, that all sorts of bottles had apparently opened spontaneously. In the bathroom, shampoo lay in a pool on the floor; in the kitchen and cellar, bleach and liquid starch. In the bedroom, a bottle of holy water was unstoppered. But all of the bottles were screw-capped – not closed with a cork or push-on cap – and none had contained a carbonated or fermentable liquid.

Three days later, at about the same time, six more bottles opened and spilt their contents. Next day, and two days after that, more bottles opened,

Parapsychologist J. Gaiter Pratt observing 12-year-old Jimmy Herrmann. The paranormal events had begun when, in the Herrmann's bathroom, kitchen and cellar, bottles – all screw caps – suddenly popped open.

Jimmy Herrmann, his 13-year-old sister Lucille and their parents James and Lucille at their Long Island home, where they experienced a poltergeist.

apparently of their own accord. James Herrmann called the police. The first to arrive was Patrolman J. Hughes and, even as he began to question the family, there came the sound of more popping bottles in the bathroom.

Detective Joseph Tozzi was assigned to the case. He reported that other objects in the Herrmann household were beginning to move. He saw a porcelain figure float through the air, and a sugar bowl dash itself against the dining-room wall. On another occasion, when all the family members were upstairs, a heavy bookcase tumbled to the floor below.

Although somewhat concerned at these bizarre events, Mr Herrmann kept his head:

'At about 10.30 a.m., I was standing in the doorway of the bathroom. All of a sudden two bottles, which had been placed on the top of the vanity table, began to move. One moved straight ahead, slowly, while the other spun to the right for a 45-degree angle. The first one fell into the sink. The second one crashed to the floor. Both bottles moved at the same time.'

Out of 68 events recorded by the Herrmanns, 23 involved bottles. All sorts of theories were advanced by the police to explain the phenomena. They suggested that high-frequency radio waves, or alternatively sonic booms caused by aircraft taking off from nearby JFK airport, might have caused the bottles to 'pop'; but an oscillograph placed in the cellar failed to detect any tremors. All the electrical circuits in the house were checked out, but without anything faulty or unusual being discovered. And then, after about a month of this mysterious activity, quite suddenly there were no more disturbances.

Unlike many cases, this seemed to be caused by a boy, Jimmy Herrmann, pictured with his family, but parapsychologists didn't believe that he was deliberately producing the effects.

COMMENTARY:

The case attracted the attention of J. B. Rhine, the director of the Parapsychology Laboratory at Duke University in North Carolina, and he sent two colleagues, Dr J. Gaither Pratt and W. G. Roll, to investigate. It had been noticed that the phenomena only occurred when 12-year-old Jimmy was in the house, and it had been suggested that they were nothing but childish pranks. But Pratt and Roll were soon convinced that Jimmy, while he might be their cause, was not deliberately producing the events. Detective Tozzi had at one time attempted to get the boy to confess that he was responsible, but he had steadfastly refused to admit anything. In any case, on many occasions the family had been together when the disturbances took place.

Pratt and Roll were unsuccessful in observing much in the way of poltergeist activity while they were on the case, and it died away during the course of the investigation. Pratt remained sure, however, that, as in so many poltergeist cases, it was the presence of a disturbed adolescent that provoked them. As he put it: 'It is within the realm of possibility that if eight million New Yorkers at one time concentrated on moving the Empire State Building, it might move a bit.'

THE EASTER VISITOR

Place: London, England

Time: Easter, 1958–1962

Victims: Graham and Vera Stringer

One night in Easter week 1958, fire broke out in Graham and Vera Stringer's London flat. It destroyed a sackful of toys belonging to their baby son Steven. There was no apparent cause for the fire; fortunately, the Stringers woke up and were able to put out the flames before they spread. On Good Friday the following year, Mrs Stringer returned home from a shopping trip to find Graham fighting a second fire in the living room. A box of presents from her mother had burst spontaneously into flames while Graham and Steven were in another room. As in the previous year, the fire was extinguished fairly quickly, although the gifts were destroyed.

Next year, on the day after Easter 1960, Vera suddenly noticed the smell of something burning. In the bedroom she found a shirt and vest belonging to Graham on fire, and a chest of drawers badly scorched.

Following this, the Stringers' fire insurance was cancelled because of their repeated claims, and they awaited Easter 1961 with trepidation. But there was no fire that year. However, they said that they had twice seen 'a grey column of fluorescent light' pass through the flat, with the sound of phantom footsteps and doors opening and closing, and later found the kitchen window broken. They came to the conclusion that they had been the victims of a poltergeist that had now left them, and irreverently christened it 'Larry'.

But the poltergeist had not finished with them. Easter 1962 arrived, and one morning Vera Stringer found the living room in flames. This was a more serious fire than any previous, and the fire brigade was called. They soon put out the flames, but, even as the Stringers were cleaning up the debris, a second blaze broke out in Steven's bedroom – fortunately the little boy was not there at the time, and there was little damage. And, to the great relief

Vera Stringer and her son Steven cleaning up after an episode of spontaneous combustion in their London home. Between 1958 and 1962 there were similar instances almost every Easter weekend.

of the Stringers, this was the last appearance of their Easter visitor.

COMMENTARY:

This is a very unusual series of events. Many cases of spontaneous combustion, without any apparent cause, have been reported over the years: among the many plausible explanations put forward have been atmospheric electrical disturbances, such as ball lightning. Nevertheless, the possibility of such phenomena recurring, in the same place and at the same season, year after year, is remote.

Steven was too young to be considered a focus for poltergeist activity – and, again, such activity is usually over a period, not just once a year. We do not know, however, whether Easter had been, at some time in the past, a time of intense emotional stress for Graham or Vera. Reporters of the case have not recorded whether this was the date of Steven's birthday (the box of presents suggests that it might have been), nor if Mrs Stringer had suffered severe trauma at the time of his birth. Possibly the subconscious recollection of such stress was sufficient to provoke the outbreak.

THE GHOST IN THE MACHINE

Place: Rosenheim, Bavaria, Germany

Time: 1967–1968

Victims: Sigmund Adam, a lawyer, and his staff

The trouble in lawyer Sigmund Adam's office, in the quiet Bavarian town of Rosenheim, began during the summer of 1967. The staff reported that the telephones were malfunctioning: calls would be interrupted by clicks, or cut off; sometimes all four telephones would ring simultaneously, but the line would be dead. The office manager, Johannes Engelhard, called in engineers from the firm that had installed the system and they, after a month in which they were unable to trace the source of the trouble, called in the Post Office.

At the beginning of October, the Post Office installed a meter in Herr Adam's office, and another at the telephone exchange, so that all calls could be recorded. In addition, Adam asked his staff to keep a personal note of all their calls. A day or two later, Adam and Engelhard were astonished to see the meter register a call when no one was using the telephone; Adam and his accountant observed the same phenomenon a fortnight later. Alerted, Adam compared the records from his own meter, the notes of his staff, and the meter records at the exchange, and discovered that dozens of undialled calls had been registered – and all of them to the 'speaking clock' on 0119.

The Post Office maintained that the calls had been made, and submitted a bill. Between 7.42 and 7.57 a.m. on 20 October 1967 alone, 46 calls were registered – equivalent to one every 20 seconds. On at least one occasion, five calls were made in the space of one minute. 'In five weeks,' Herr Adam reported, 'the speaking clock was connected between 500 and 600 times – in one day, 80 times.' He insisted that the Post Office equipment was faulty, they insisted that the records were genuine.

The matter might have been dismissed as a malfunction, and some kind of agreement reached between Adam and the Post Office, if other remarkable events had not begun to occur. On 20 October, the office fluorescent lights went out with

In investigating the Rosenheim case, parapsychologist Hans Bender focused on the law firm's 18-year-old clerk Annemarie Schneider. She subsequently lost her job – and the phenomena stopped.

a bang. A local electrician was called, and found that each tube had been twisted in its socket and disconnected. He had just finished replacing the tubes when there was another bang, and he found the tubes again twisted and disconnected. The staff then told him that the automatic fuses had been ejecting without apparent cause, sometimes on all four circuits at once.

The electrician checked all the office wiring and equipment, and found no faults. He suggested that the electricity supply must be responsible, and a recording meter was installed in the circuit: it showed inexplicable surges in current. The fluorescent tubes continued to give trouble, and in November they were replaced by standard light bulbs: the next day these began to explode. By the end of the month, the entire Rosenheim electricity supply had been checked, and Adam's office connected to an independent generator-truck parked outside the office; but, inside, bulbs continued to explode, and fuses to eject. And then the lamps began to swing.

As Adam later commented: 'We leapt repeatedly up and down the floor overhead to try to make the lamps swing – without success. The traffic outside was also watched carefully, and tests were made for electrostatic charges, but none was found.' Some lamps swung so violently that they smashed into the ceiling, cracking the plaster. And on the morning of 11 December paintings hanging in the offices began to turn, one rotating through nearly a full circle, wrapping its cord around the hook.

The electricity company's engineer decided to call in two physicists, Dr Karger of the Max Planck Institute of Plasma Physics, and Dr Zicha of Munich University. After investigating every possibility, they came to the conclusion that some undetectable force was at work, distorting the operation of the measuring equipment itself. This would also explain how the telephone had sent pulses down the line without the dial being used. They also established that the phenomena occurred only when the staff were in the office, but they concluded that fraud and trickery were impossible. The time had come to call in the parapsychologists.

Hans Bender of the Freiburg Institute of Parapsychology was contacted, and his team turned their investigations to the staff: Engelhard, and the two clerks, 17-year-old Gustel Hüber and 18-year-old Annemarie Schneider. Soon attention centred on Annemarie: she was very tense, and reacted hysterically to the phenomena. She was given a few days' leave, and the phenomena ceased – only to resume even more violently on her return: pictures swung and fell, pages were torn from the calendar, and desk drawers slid out and had to be wedged shut with heavy stools.

The police also took an interest in the occurrences, and Officer Wendel was sure that he would eventually prove that Annemarie was physically responsible. His assurance was severely shaken, however, when a heavy oak cabinet moved over a foot, and could only be replaced with the help of two strong policemen. Later the same day, the cabinet moved again, chairs shifted, and a table jerked sideways while an astounded visitor was sitting on it. Reluctantly, Adam told Annemarie that she must leave: she never returned – and neither did the poltergeist.

COMMENTARY:

Hans Bender invited Annemarie to Freiburg so that he could carry out laboratory tests; after some hesitation, she agreed to spend a week there at the end of January 1968. Attempts to get her to influence equipment in the laboratory were unsuccessful, but Bender also had her put through an exhaustive psychological assessment. The psychologist, John Mischo, concluded that

Annemarie suffered from frustrated rage: she was unable to tolerate denial, but suppressed her aggression. She was unhappy in Adam's office, and Bender hypothesized that the speaking clock had first been contacted as a result of her constant desire to know when she could leave for home.

Subsequent discreet enquiries established that Annemarie had had a succession of jobs after leaving Adam's employment, but her reputation had followed her, and she was invariably dismissed if anything inexplicable occurred. In 1975, she told a BBC television team: 'I worked in Regenfelchen in a paper factory, and there was an accident when a man was killed. The workers who knew who I was said: "That woman is responsible for the man's death."' She moved to Munich, and there, in the anonymity of the big city, no further phenomena were reported.

It has been suggested that the severity of the poltergeist events was heightened by the attention given to them. Hans Bender pointed out that they were observed over a period of several months by more than 40 witnesses in all, including electrical engineers, physicists and the police – but nobody was able to give an explanation, other than to suggest that Annemarie, somehow, was the emotional cause.

THE ENFIELD POLTERGEIST

Place: Enfield, north London, England

Time: 1977–1978

Victims: Peggy Hodgson, her 11-year-old daughter Janet, and three other children

The case of the Enfield poltergeist has been recorded in detail by Guy Lyon Playfair, a member of the Society for Psychical Research, and it is of particular interest, because a number of photographs of the incidents – admittedly of somewhat doubtful quality – were taken during the course of the manifestation.

On the evening of 31 August 1977, Peggy Hodgson, a single mother, was putting her 11-year-old daughter Janet and one of her sons to bed when both children remarked that something was making 'a shuffling noise'. With astonishment, she saw that a heavy chest of drawers, well out of reach of the children's feet, was moving along the floor. She pushed it back, but it moved again, and this time she was unable to replace it – and then came four loud knocks on the wall.

Shocked, she ran to call for the help of her neighbours, Vic and Peggy Nottingham. Vic and his son searched the house, but found nothing, though they heard knocking on the wall of the staircase. The police were called, and in the presence of WPC Carolyn Heeps, who later signed a written statement, one of the chairs in the living room was seen to slide, just as the chest had done earlier.

The next day, children's marbles and toy bricks began to fly about the house; many, when picked up, were found to be hot. After three days, the distraught Mrs Hodgson could think of nothing better than to telephone the *Daily Mirror* newspaper.

Late in the evening of 4 September, the newspaper's photographer, Graham Morris, was just pressing the shutter of his camera – with everybody clearly visible through his viewfinder – when a toy brick hit his forehead so hard that the bruise was still visible a week later. His colleague, senior reporter George Fallows, was sufficiently impressed by Morris's account to inform the Society of Psychical Research. Maurice Grosse, a new (and relatively inexperienced) member of the Society, volunteered to undertake an investigation.

On 8 September, Grosse witnessed a variety of typical poltergeist phenomena. A child's marble was hurled at him; a door opened and closed by itself three

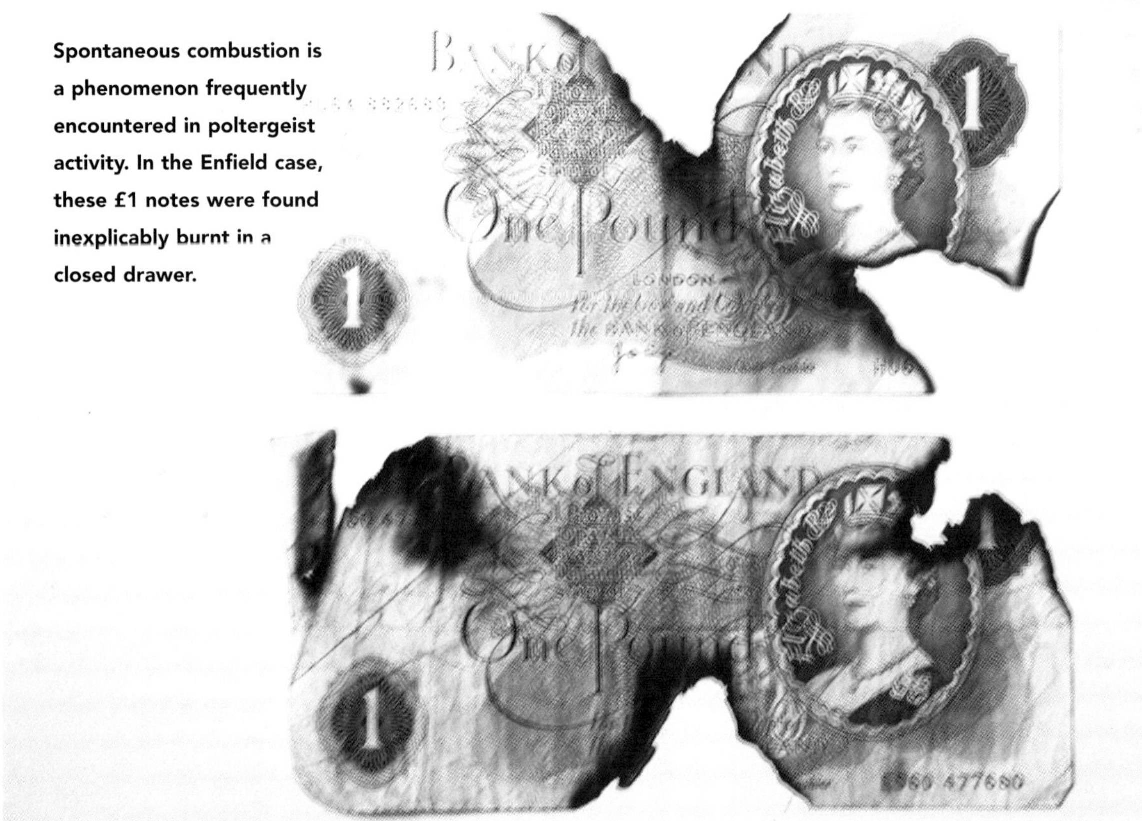

Spontaneous combustion is a phenomenon frequently encountered in poltergeist activity. In the Enfield case, these £1 notes were found inexplicably burnt in a closed drawer.

or four times; and a shirt rose from a pile of laundry placed on the kitchen table, and fell to the floor.

Extensive media reports during the next few days persuaded Guy Lyon Playfair, another member of the Society of Psychical Research, to join Grosse in the investigation. The knocking on walls and floors had continued, and both men found that it would respond to questions in the traditional way, giving one rap for 'no' and two for 'yes'. One evening, Grosse asked how long the 'entity' had been in the house, and received a reply of 53 raps, which was recorded on tape while all the family was in full view.

Soon after, however, the raps came in a meaningless way, and Grosse exclaimed: 'Are you having a game with me?' A second later, a box of toys and cushions rose from a corner of the room, flew through the air for a distance of about two metres (eight feet), and hit Grosse on the forehead. Playfair managed to record the sounds of many incidents on tape, although he often found that tapes were broken, or inexplicably wiped clean. But attempts to obtain photographic evidence were less successful. A team from the electrical company Pye brought a television camera sensitive to infrared, with which they hoped to carry out some remote monitoring inside the children's bedroom, but the machine malfunctioned without any apparent cause.

Graham Morris, however, managed to take two high-speed sequences with his motor-driven camera, one of two pillows in motion, the other of bedclothes apparently being pulled from Janet, while a curtain twists into a tight spiral. Other photographs reveal the havoc caused by the movement of large pieces of furniture.

The events that are alleged to have occurred on 15 December 1977 remain the most extraordinary of all, as they appear to be supported by several independent witnesses. Significantly, this day was the date of Janet's first menstruation. For some days previously, she had begun speaking with a hoarse male voice, a voice over which she claimed she had no control. It sometimes related information – such as the manner and place of death of a former occupant of the house – of which Janet should have had no knowledge.

David Robertson, from the physics department of Birkbeck College, London, had joined the team, and had handed Janet a large and heavy sofa cushion and asked her to make it 'disappear'. At this time, a local tradesman, who did not know the Hodgsons and did not believe what he had heard about the

Strangely burnt items from the Enfield case. Fire is one of the more dangerous of poltergeist activities, but fortunately in this case, the fires were self-extinguished or relatively easily dealt with.

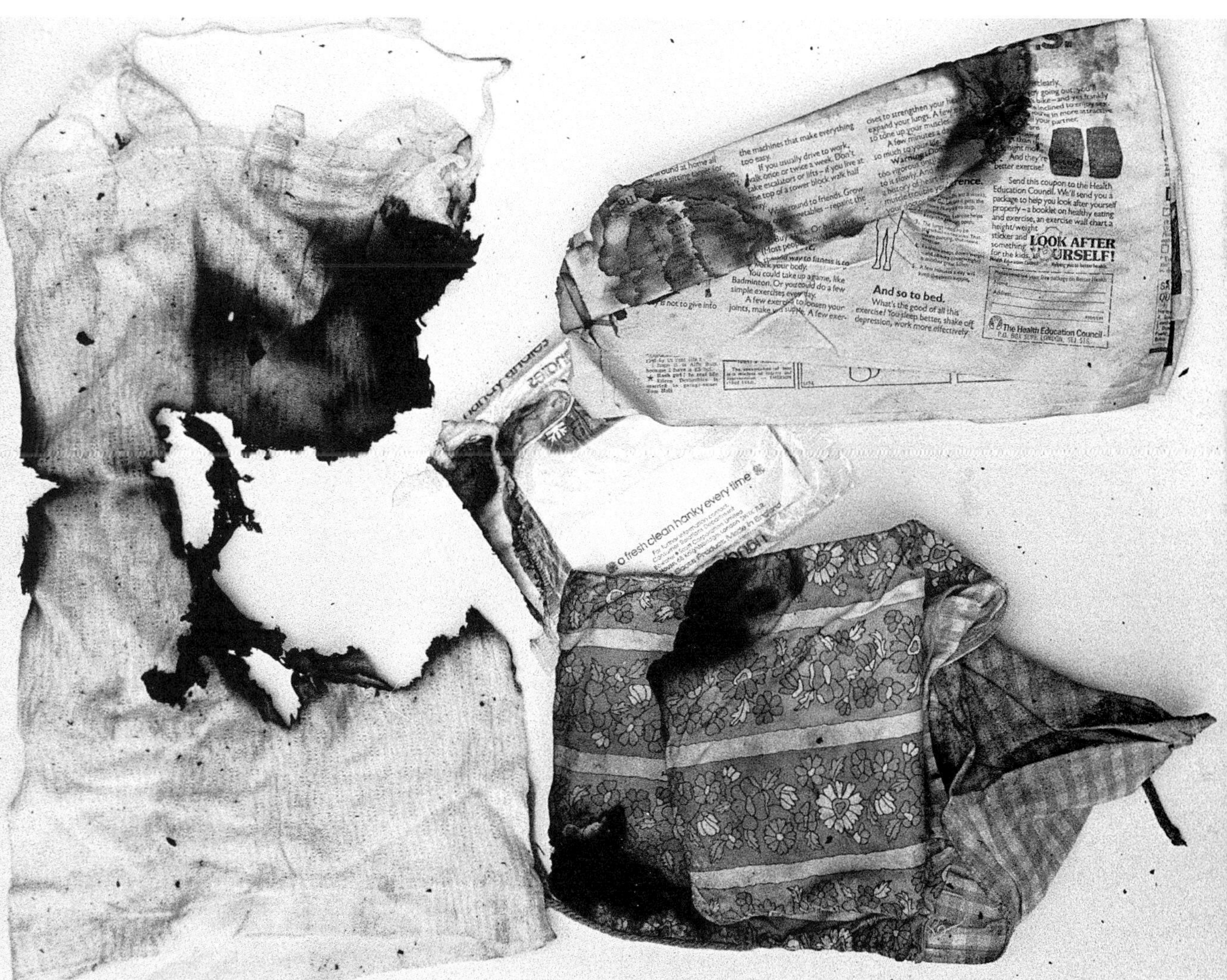

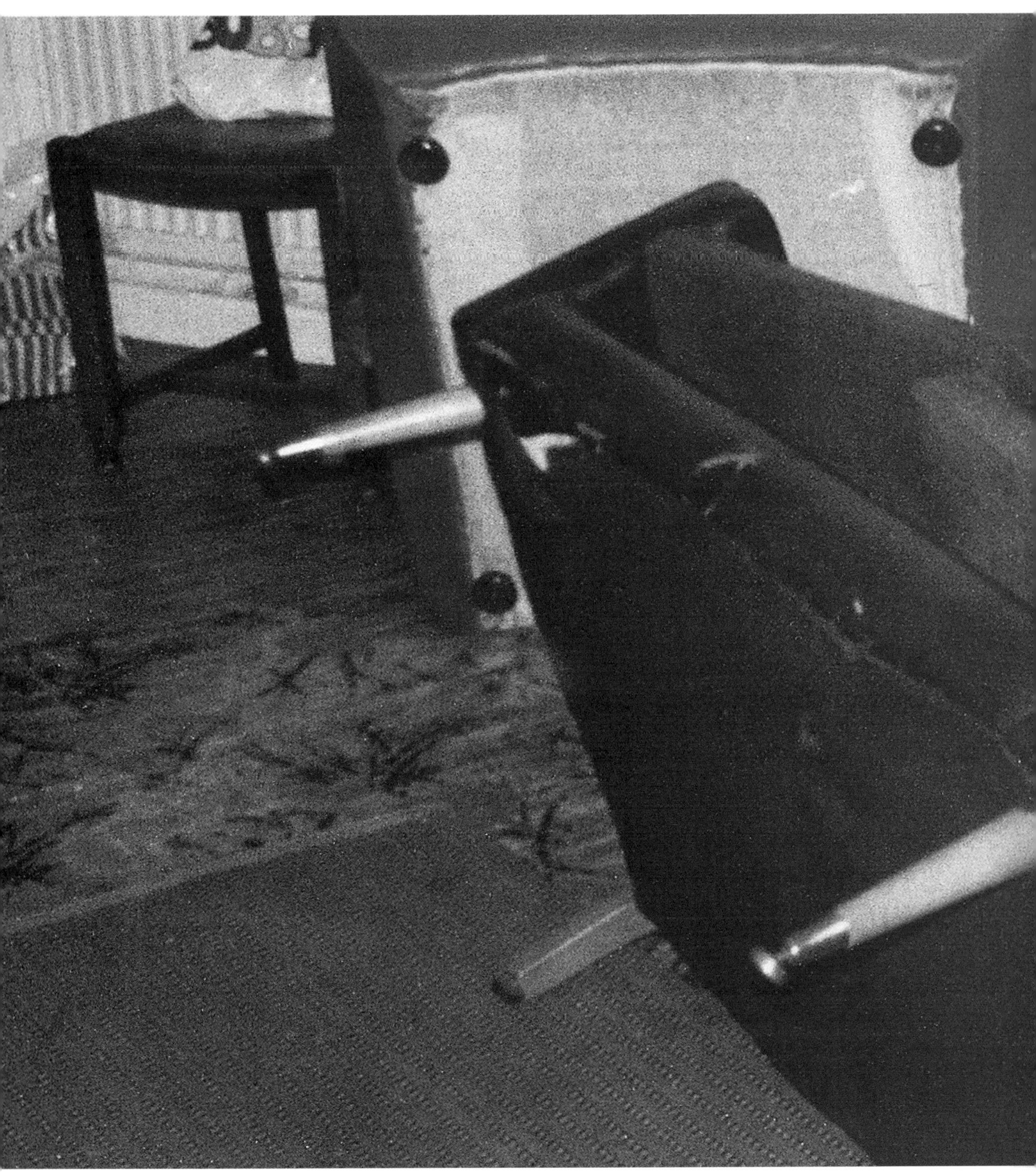

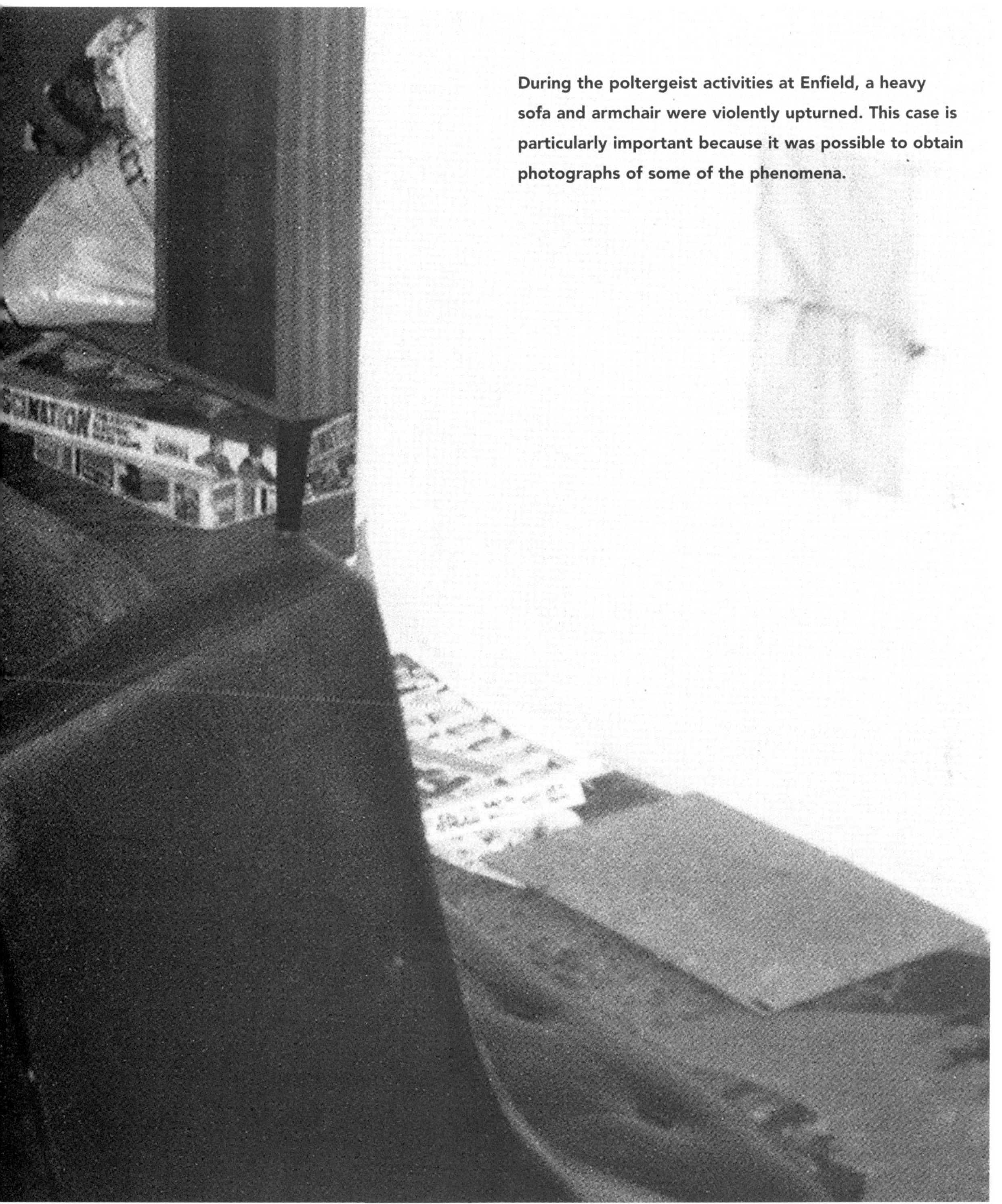

During the poltergeist activities at Enfield, a heavy sofa and armchair were violently upturned. This case is particularly important because it was possible to obtain photographs of some of the phenomena.

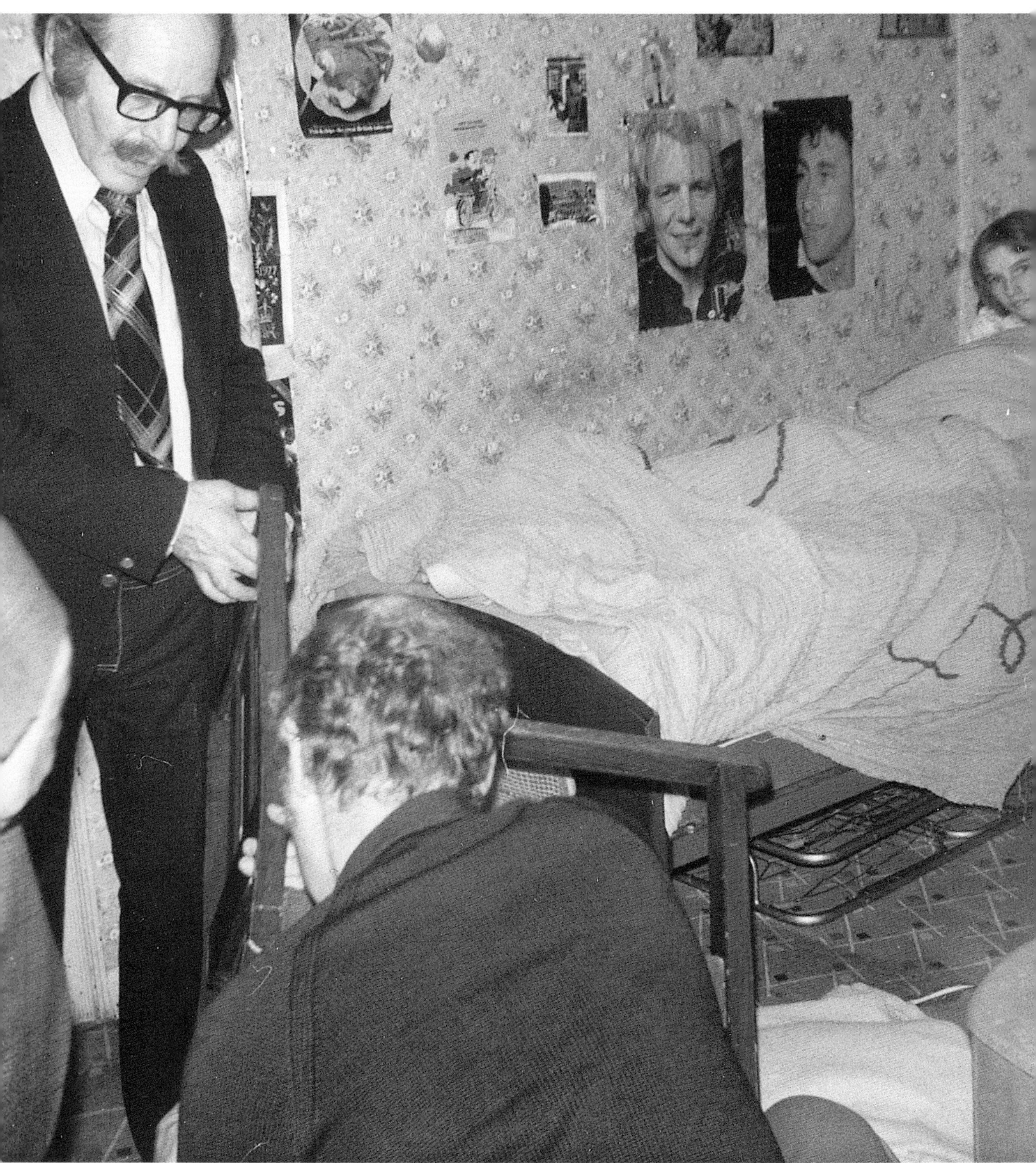

manifestations, saw a large red cushion on the roof of the Hodgsons' house. And he testified that, as he passed the house, he saw in amazement, through the upper bedroom window, Janet 'floating horizontally across the room'.

Mrs Hazel Short, who was on school-crossing duty across the road from the house, also testified that she had seen the girl 'definitely horizontal'. From the angle of view of these two observers, the investigators calculated that Janet must have been at least 70 cm (28 inches) above her bed.

The disturbances continued for some time, but ceased around October 1978. Four years later, however, Professor J. B. Hasted, head of physics at Birkbeck College, carried out a laboratory investigation designed to show whether Janet was truly capable of levitation.

She was seated in a chair placed on a specially constructed platform that was attached to a chart recorder. Any change in weight would be shown in a movement of the recorder. Although Janet sat perfectly still during the experiment, the chart showed that, over a period of some 30 seconds, she had steadily lost two pounds (one kg) in weight.

Professor Hasted was at pains to point out that the experiment was not evidence of levitation, but his results remain inexplicable.

COMMENTARY:

Guy Lyon Playfair's account of the Enfield poltergeist has come under severe criticism from some other members of the SPR. In particular, a council member of the society, Anita Gregory, who visited the house in Enfield, was convinced that all she saw and heard there was the result of pranks played by the Hodgson children. In her opinion, the early phenomena could have been genuine, but the intense interest shown by Grosse (as an inexperienced investigator), Playfair, and, above all, the media, persuaded the children to satisfy them by playing tricks.

The Enfield Haunting: Maurice Grosse (left) and Guy Lyon Playfair examine the bedroom furniture, while Janet looks on. In all the photographs, she appears the only unconcerned member of the family.

Janet was the principal focus for the events. Much was made at the time of alleged forces that hurled Janet from her bed, but, as Anita Gregory pointed out, the bedroom walls were clearly decorated with certificates testifying to Janet's athletic ability. And it is noteworthy that, in all the photographs taken during the manifestations, it is Janet who smiles knowingly.

'And what,' asked Ms Gregory, 'of the video recording that David Robertson took before Janet knew he was doing so, and in which she can be seen bending a spoon and trying to bend a thick metal bar in a thoroughly normal manner – by force – and then bouncing up and down on the bed, making little flapping movements with both hands?' It is not known whether she could bounce up 70 cm (28 inches), but the case rests.

'FLYING KILLER TELEPHONES'

Place: Columbus, Ohio, USA

Time: 1984

Victims: John and Joan Resch

At 9 a.m. one Saturday in March 1984, all the lights suddenly went on in a modest family home in Columbus, Ohio. John and Joan Resch, their 14-year-old adopted daughter Tina, and their four foster children, were sure that nobody had touched a switch – let alone all the switches in the house.

When the local electrical contractor, Bruce Claggett, arrived, he was confident that the problem would prove to be a faulty circuit breaker, but: 'I was up there three hours,' he reported, 'and the lights were just turning themselves on all over the place.' He tried fixing the switches in the off position with tape, but: 'as fast as I would tape them in the down position, they'd come back on.'

By Saturday evening, other manifestations were beginning. Objects such as lamps, wall hangings and brass candlesticks moved through the air; an upstairs shower ran on its own; the hands of clocks began turning faster than normal. Near midnight, the Resches called the local police, but they confessed themselves powerless. Next day, wine glasses shattered, eggs leapt from the stove top

James Randi, stage magician and debunker of much alleged supernatural phenomena, dismissed the Tina Resch story as the 'attack of the flying killer telephones'. He believed that Resch had simply staged the occurrences by pulling unseen telephone cords.

and smashed on the ceiling, and knives flew from drawers. The focus of the disturbances seemed to be Tina, who was struck several times by flying objects. A chair tumbled after her as she crossed the living room, before it became wedged in the doorway. The only respite came when she left the house for church.

By Monday morning, the house was a shambles of broken glass and upset furniture. Reporter Mike Harden and photographer Fred Shannon, from the *Columbus Dispatch*, arrived. Harden reported that Tina cried: 'I just want it to stop!'

'But even as she spoke, a telephone near her leaped through the air. She replaced it not once, but a half-dozen times. Each time, as stunned visitors watched it, it would again fling itself across the room. A cup of coffee flipped from a nearby table onto Tina's lap and then smashed against the fireplace. She moved to a love seat. An afghan rug on the floor lifted itself into the air and flopped over her.'

Shannon was able to photograph the flying telephone, and the picture appeared in the next edition of the newspaper, sparking off a national sensation. Reporters from newspapers, radio and television came crowding to the Resch home, in the hope of seeing further phenomena. W. G. Roll, by then director of the Psychical Research Institute in North Carolina, flew to the scene, and witnessed a picture falling, and his own tape recorder flying a distance of two metres (seven feet).

Like all poltergeist events, these disturbances eventually came to an end. But the controversy concerning them did not.

COMMENTARY:

James Randi, the stage magician who has devoted much of his time to investigating – and usually debunking – supernatural phenomena, took a close interest in the case. The Resches had barred him from the house, but he was able to gain access to the roll of film taken by the *Dispatch* news photographer. Only one frame taken from the film had been published by the newspaper, but Randi revealed that other frames showed Tina's hands clearly in a position to reach the telephone cord, or even the instrument itself. The magician jokingly named the disturbances 'the attack of the flying killer telephones'.

Further damaging evidence emerged later. A television camera had unintentionally been left running during one sequence of events. It showed Tina grasping the cord of a table lamp and pulling it towards her, while letting out a cry of alarm. When she was questioned, Tina said that she had become exasperated by the continued intrusion of interviewers, and had hoped that they would leave her to herself once they had been satisfied by some apparently inexplicable phenomenon.

This is another case of poltergeist activity focused on a pubescent girl. It seems impossible that Tina could deliberately have produced all the phenomena, but the credulity of untrained observers is notorious, and at no time was the girl under strict conditions of observation. We have, however, the testimony of W. G. Roll, who was very experienced in occurrences of this kind. Whether Tina consciously or unconsciously provoked the events, it seems that she was unable to control them. As she said: 'I just want it to stop.'

Although the events did stop, Tina's life remained troubled. In 1992, her three-year-old daughter Amber was found dead, believed to have been beaten to death. Tina, now twice divorced and calling herself Christina Boyer, and her boyfriend of three months, David Herrin, were charged with the child's murder. To avoid the risk of receiving the death sentence, Tina entered a plea bargain while protesting her innocence and was sentenced to a life sentence plus 20 years with the possibility of parole. Herrin was convicted of cruelty to children and was released in 2011.

The photograph of 14-year-old Tina Resch and 'flying killer telephones' as it appeared in the *Columbus Dispatch* in 1984. Parapsychologist W. G. Roll believed that Resch had telekinetic powers.

In 2004, W. G. Roll published *Unleashed – Of Poltergeists and Murder: The Curious Story of Tina Resch*. He thought that she was innocent in the death of Amber, but, 20 years after the events that had brought the name of Tina Resch into the news, he stood by his belief that she had telekinetic powers.

A HAUNTED BED

Time: 1998

Place: Savannah, Georgia, USA

Reporter: Al Cobb

For the first two nights he slept in it, 14-year-old Jason Cobb loved the 19th-century antique bed that his parents, Al, an antique dealer, and Lila, had bought for him. But on the third night something disturbing happened: Jason awoke to the feeling of

two invisible elbows pushing into the pillow beside him and the sense of a cold breath on his face.

At first, his parents dismissed Jason's concerns as a dream, but the following night Jason opened the door to his room to find a picture of his grandfather that had been on the bedside table now face down. Perhaps a draught had knocked it over, we might think. But the next day, Jason found the picture on the bed and assorted items from around the room, including a conch shell, a dinosaur made from small shells and a plaster cast of a bird, arranged around it.

Al decided to communicate with the spirit, asking its name and age, and, when it didn't respond to his questions, he left crayons and paper on the bed. Fifteen minutes later, Al returned to find scrawled on the paper 'Danny' and '7'.

In the following weeks, Al learned that Danny's mother had died in the bed in 1899 and that he didn't want anyone else sleeping in it. Jason was no longer using the bed, but he lay down on it one day to test the reaction. Soon a wall-hanging flew across the room, narrowly missing him. There were similar occurrences, such as kitchen drawers suddenly opening and furniture being knocked over.

Jason soon claimed to be in contact with other spirits in the house. One was 'Uncle Sam', who told the boy that his daughter was buried underneath the house and that Sam was there to claim her. Another was a young girl called 'Gracie', who is thought to be Gracie Watson, buried in nearby Bonaventure Cemetery, where there is a statue of her.

COMMENTARY:

Parapsychologist Dr. Andrew Nichols, head of the Florida Society for Parapsychological Research and a psychologist at Santa Fe College, Gainesville, Florida, investigated the case at the Cobb house. He found that an unusual configuration of wiring in the walls of Jason's room had caused a very strong electromagnetic field. He dismissed the importance of the bed itself, but that by moving the bed against the wall, the electromagnetic energy hidden there had 'charged a psychic ability that the boy already had'. The electromagnetism coming through the bedroom walls had switched on Jason's psychic powers.

But for Nichols to believe that there was a poltergeist in the house, he would have had to witness it himself or to have recorded it on film, which he did not, though he did not dismiss the possibility of a poltergeist.

CHAPTER 9

THE VANISHING HITCHHIKER & OTHER URBAN MYTHS

Usually told as having happened to 'a friend of a friend', urban myths are a new kind of ghost story and still include a supernatural element. Seemingly convincing, these contemporary accounts are often no more than updated forms of much older tales.

THE GHOST IN THE LIFT

Place: Paris, France

Time: 1893

Reporter: Lord Dufferin

Frederick Hamilton-Temple-Blackwood, First Marquess of Dufferin and Ava, led a distinguished diplomatic career between 1860 and 1896, culminating in his posting as British Ambassador to Paris for six years. He was a great raconteur, and one of his after-dinner stories particularly impressed his teenage nephew Harold Nicolson.

In 1883, Lord Dufferin was staying at a great house near Tullamore, County Offaly, Ireland. One night he awoke in bed in terror: strange and horrifying noises were coming from the grounds beyond his window, heart-rending sobs, more animal than human. He rose from the bed and peered out – and saw, emerging from the shadow of the trees into the moonlight, the figure of a man bent double beneath the weight of a coffin.

The window opened on to a terrace: Dufferin flung it wide and ran out, shouting for the man to stop. The figure halted and turned its head, revealing a hideous countenance so distorted with pain and hatred that for a moment Dufferin stopped in his tracks; then he dashed forward again – running right through the figure, which immediately vanished.

Dufferin, shaken, returned to his room and wrote an account of his experience, before falling once more into a troubled sleep. Next morning he consulted his host and fellow guests, but no one could offer an explanation – not even a story of a local ghost. For years, Dufferin believed that it must all have been a nightmare.

A lonely road stretches into the distance. It is in such a landscape that the vanishing hitchhiker of urban myth appears, accepts a lift from a motorist, and, later, mysteriously disappears.

The First Marquess of Dufferin and Ava. His after-dinner stories gave rise to a persistent myth that spread, first from Ireland to France, and then to the United States, and back again.

Ten years later, when Lord Dufferin was ambassador in Paris, he attended a diplomatic reception at the Grand Hotel accompanied by his secretary. They stood waiting with a crowd of other guests for the lift, but when the doors opened he staggered back, pulling his secretary with him, and refused to enter the lift. The face of the lift attendant was identical, in every feature, with that of the ghastly figure that he had encountered in Ireland.

Other guests ignored him, and crowded into the lift, which began its slow upward climb. But, even as Dufferin turned away to find the hotel manager's office and enquire about its attendant, there came the horrifying sound of cables snapping, and the lift, with its human cargo, plunged down the shaft, killing all its occupants. No one came forward later to claim the mangled remains of the attendant's body; in fact, no one knew who he was – he had only been hired that day. But Lord Dufferin knew that somehow his vision at Tullamore 10 years earlier had saved his life.

COMMENTARY:

Lord Dufferin's nephew, Harold Nicolson, grew up to become a writer, and told this story in one of his books. But the first published account came in 1920 from the French psychologist R. de Maratray, who had heard it from Nicolson, and incorporated it into a book, *Death and its Mystery* (1923).

Shortly after the book's publication, its contents were investigated by Paul Heuze, a journalist on the Paris magazine *l'Opinion*. He showed that the book was full of unsubstantiated tales and hearsay and, in particular, that the story of Lord Dufferin's miraculous escape was unsupported by facts. The accident at the Grand Hotel had occurred in 1878 – five years before Dufferin's supposed experience in Ireland, and at a time when he was Governor General of Canada – and there had been only one fatality, that of a young woman.

More facts came to light in November 1949, when a Louis Wolfe of New York wrote to the Society for Psychical Research in London, asking for details of the society's 'Dufferin investigation'. The secretary of the SPR replied that the society had never investigated the case, but then wrote to Lord Dufferin's granddaughter concerning the matter. She replied that the story was one that her grandfather used to tell – but about someone else. The story was of some unnamed friend who, while staying at Glamis Castle in Scotland, had been visited by a hearse driven by a man with a distorted face.

Further investigation turned up a similar tale in the issue of the Spiritualist paper *Light* for 16 April 1892. The editor, Rev. Stainton Moses, wrote: 'It has been communicated to me by a personal friend, and is both authentic and trustworthy.' The story was of a young woman who dreamt that she heard a knocking at her house door and, looking out, saw a hearse with a strange-looking driver, who asked her: 'Are you not ready yet?' Some weeks later, she was about to enter a lift in a large City warehouse when she was amazed to recognize the face of the attendant, who asked her: 'Are you not ready yet, Miss?' She refused to enter the lift, and 'it only reached to the next floor, when the machinery gave way, the lift being smashed to pieces, and the man killed'.

By various means the story spread, the details gradually changing. It eventually appeared in the American publication *The Progressive Thinker*, from which it was once again reprinted in *Light* on 9 February 1907. Now it involved a Miss Gray from Washington State, who was on a visit to Chicago, and planned to go shopping in one of the city's new department stores. The night before, she saw an unknown face at her bedroom window, some six metres (20 feet) above the ground; on going to the window, she saw a hearse in the street, with her visitor sitting in the driver's seat and beckoning to her.

Next day, when Miss Gray was in the department store, she was just about to enter a lift when the same man beckoned to her, saying there was room for one more. She stood back, however, and the lift 'started down, stuck, and dropped four storeys, killing two of its passengers and injuring everyone else in the car'.

The way in which versions of this story have continued to proliferate exemplifies the powerful attraction of the urban myth. In this particular instance, note how the original story – before Lord Dufferin assumed it to himself to amuse his dinner guests – was already about 'a friend'.

FLYING DEATH

Place: Shallufa, Egypt

Time: 1942

Reporter: Wing-Commander G. A. Potter

At the time of his disturbing experiences, Wing-Commander G. A. Potter was an RAF Squadron-Leader, with ground administrative duties, with a bomber group occupied in torpedo and mine-laying operations in the eastern Mediterranean during World War II. As he put it 30 years later:

'Somehow I had developed the ability to "see" which of [the men] were going to die. I remember one night the adjutant came and told me that a Canadian pilot was drunk in the officers' mess and wouldn't leave the bar. I suddenly realized that he was doomed and said: "Leave the poor devil alone – he's only got two days left, and probably knows it." Two days later he was killed.'

Potter told himself that it was a coincidence: squadrons were bound to lose men on bombing missions. 'But too many times I had known beyond doubt that a man would die soon and, hunch or not, my predictions as to "who" and "when" were always uncannily accurate.'

Then came his most horrifying vision. As Potter walked late one night into the mess, he saw the Wing-Commander of one torpedo squadron surrounded by a group of his officer aircrew: 'They were a good, happy, crowd and I liked them: their commanding officer was tall, good-looking, with curly gold hair and a ready smile. He was gallant and deservedly popular... The station armament officer, Flying Officer Lamb, came in and joined me... I got him a drink.

'As I handed it to him, there was a burst of laughter from the group on my left, and I glanced toward them. Then I saw the head and shoulders of the Wing-Commander moving ever so slowly in a bottomless depth of blue-blackness. His lips were drawn back from his teeth in a dreadful grin; he had eye sockets but no eyes; the flesh of his face was dully blotched in greenish, purplish shadows, with shreds peeling off near his left ear.'

Potter gradually became aware that Flying Officer Lamb was speaking to him – Potter, Lamb said, looked as if he'd seen a ghost. Potter told him that he *had* seen a ghost, and pointed out the Wing-Commander, but Lamb could see nothing. Potter wondered whether he should report his vision to the Group Captain, but realized that the Wing-Commander would refuse to be withdrawn from the forthcoming operation. 'In any case,' he said, 'I am convinced that the decision not to interfere was already made for me as part of a preordained sequence of events.'

Next morning, the torpedo squadron flew forward. And on the following day Potter was told that the Wing-Commander's plane had been shot down –

but that he and his crew had been seen getting into their inflatable dinghies. 'I felt an enormous sense of relief,' said Potter, 'but my elation was short-lived. They searched and searched, but no one ever saw [them] again. And then I knew the meaning of what I had seen. The blue-black nothingness was the Mediterranean Sea at night; and he was floating somewhere in it, dead, with just his head and shoulders held up by his Mae West [life jacket].'

COMMENTARY:

This story is included here, not because any doubt is to be thrown on Wing-Commander Potter's own account, but because it is typical of many tales that circulated during the war, and which, because of their similarity, must be considered as the source of a particular urban myth. The heightened strain of wartime operations may very well have resulted in paranormal visions of this kind, but subsequently the stories have spread, multiplied, and been embroidered to a point where their origin can no longer be traced.

AN ICE-COLD DANCER

Place: A coastal area in the USA

Time: 1950s

Reporters: Debby Creecy and Sharon McPartland

Joy Hendrix, her husband, and a male friend, set out one evening from Savannah, Georgia, to drive to the beach, where they intended to go dancing. The road was long and straight and, as they drove, they saw a girl standing about a half a mile (800 metres) ahead, apparently hoping for a lift. 'The wind was blowing, and her long blonde hair seemed to flow with the wind along with the soft material of her white dress,' Joy later related. The driver pulled to a stop beside the girl, and she asked if they would give her a ride to the beach.

Although it was summer it was not a warm night and, while the others in the car had wraps, the girl wore only a sleeveless dress. 'We had not driven more than a mile (1.5km) before she said she was hot, and wondered if it was all right to lower the window,' Joy remembered. 'We felt that something must be wrong with her… but of course we went along with her, and she did this in a jovial manner.' They asked her if she would like to join them at the dancehall, and she accepted, saying she 'would love to'. Before dancing, the group decided to take a stroll on the pier, but wondered whether the girl might find it too cool. She insisted that she would find it refreshing, because she felt rather warm.

The party returned to the dancehall and, after the male friend had danced with the girl, she excused herself for a moment. While she was gone, he looked puzzled: 'Something's wrong,' he said. 'As soon as I took her hand to dance, it was just like holding a piece of ice. She isn't warm, she's cold.' Joy's husband reported the same after he had danced with the girl.

Soon afterwards, the Hendrixes decided to return home, and the girl said she would leave with them. The friend, who found her charming, asked for her address, which she gave him, as well as her name, Rose White, and said that he was welcome to call on her at some time. She insisted, however, on being put down at the spot where they had picked her up, and refused to let Mr Hendrix drive to her home.

The following day, the Hendrix's friend was anxious to see Rose again, and persuaded them to drive out to the address he had been given. 'We got to the place where we picked her up,' said Joy, 'and, sure enough, this was the name of the street that she lived on.' They drove up the road for about a mile before coming to the number Rose had given, but

The tale of Rose White is another version of the vanishing hitchhiker urban myth. But rather than being a story heard about 'a friend of a friend', we have the accounts of those it happened to.

found that it was a convent. They wondered whether she had slipped out secretly, and if this was the reason she had been unwilling for them to drive her home, but decided to enquire after her.

The sister who answered the door looked at them with concern, and invited them in. 'When did you know Rose White?' she asked. When they told her that they had met the girl only the night before, she took down an old photo album from a shelf and asked them to look through it for a picture of Rose. They quickly found one, at which the sister said that they were not the first to come looking for Rose, and she would show them where she was. She led them out again to the car, and directed them along the road to a nearby cemetery. There they walked between the graves, until they came to a stone, and on it was the name, 'Rose White.'

The sister explained that Rose had died, many years before, on the day of her graduation from high school, and was buried on the same date as the previous day. 'Yes,' she said, 'Rose White has been seen three other times, and it's always on the date of the day she was buried. She doesn't come back but once every 15 years.'

COMMENTARY:

This is a relatively early example of the contemporary form of the hitchhiker story, and interesting in that it is allegedly, like the accounts that follow, a direct report from one of those who had the experience. In 1971, Joy Hendrix was living in Metter, Candler County, Georgia, and her account was recorded by Debby Creecy and Sharon McPartland.

In his book *The Vanishing Hitchhiker: American Urban Legends and their Meanings* (1981), the folklorist J. H. Brunvand casts doubt on the validity of most, or all, of these stories. He traces their origin through several generations, and asserts that it is impossible to discover those who are supposed to have had the reported experience. He produces persuasive evidence to support his argument, but it would be interesting to know his reaction to the stories reproduced here, in which actual names, dates and locations are given.

Nevertheless, it must be admitted that the germ of the tale appears in many widely separated cultures. In Hawaii, for instance, the phenomenon is associated with Pele, the goddess of the volcano Mauna Loa, who appears – and disappears – in the guise of an old woman carrying a basket beside the road. In Malaysia there is the *langsuyar*, a vampire spirit that assumes the form of an attractive girl who hitches a lift on a lonely road. Soon after entering the car, she flies into the air, with terrifying shrieks.

The stories that follow are of a much more mundane character, and are supported by considerable circumstantial evidence. The similarity of the form is, however, significant. Perhaps this is a case of an archetypal myth: the reporters have had some kind of experience, but have subconsciously shaped its telling to conform to the archetype.

THE UNIONDALE APPARITION

Place: Near Uniondale, South Africa

Time: 1978

Reporters: Dawie van Jaarsveld and others

Early one evening in the spring of 1978, Corporal van Jaarsveld of the South African army was riding his motorcycle along the Barandas–Willowmore road near Uniondale, on his way to visit his girlfriend at Louterwater Farm. He was listening through earphones to the radio as he drove. Ahead of him along the road he saw an attractive dark-haired girl, wearing dark trousers and a blue top, who was obviously hoping for a lift. He stopped and looked round cautiously, in case she was a decoy for a mugging, but, seeing that the surroundings were clear, he offered her the pillion seat, and gave her the spare crash helmet that he always carried, and an extra earplug so that she, too, could listen to the radio.

After a few miles, Van Jaarsveld noticed that the rear of the motorcycle was bumping strangely, and looked round to find his passenger missing. He stopped and rode back, fearful that the girl might have fallen off. But there was no sign of her anywhere, neither on the road nor in the open

Corporal Dawie van Jaarsveld gave a lift to a young woman near Uniondale, South Africa. She disappeared from the seat of his motorcycle at high speed, leaving no trace.

countryside on either side – and the spare helmet was attached in its usual place.

The incident soon became news, and two local investigators, Cynthia Hind and David Barritt, looked into the matter. Hind visited a cafe in Uniondale, whose proprietress confirmed that Van Jaarsveld had called there shortly after the incident, and had been deeply disturbed. At Louterwater Farm, too, the inhabitants attested to the corporal's distracted state. Barritt showed a photograph to Van Jaarsveld, which he immediately recognized. It was of 22-year-old Maria Roux, who had been killed in the early hours of 12 April 1968 when a car driven by her fiancé had veered off the road.

It then turned out that, two years previously, Anton Le Grange had had a similar experience. He had stopped to give a lift to a young woman, who had asked to be taken to an address that could not subsequently be verified, and who had disappeared during the journey. Le Grange said he had heard a scream from the back of the car, and had turned round to see the right-hand rear door swinging open. Remarkably, a PC Potgeiter had been travelling behind Le Grange's car, and, he too, had seen the door opening, without any person being involved.

COMMENTARY:

This case, unusually, offers a number of independent witnesses, and a plausible identification of the apparition. Almost identical experiences have been reported by several other travellers along the Uniondale road.

When Van Jaarsveld was shown a photo of Maria Roux, right, he immediately identified her. She had been killed in a road accident near Uniondale 10 years previously.

A PHANTOM, OR A CHANGE OF MIND?

Place: Stanbridge, Bedfordshire, England

Time: October 1979

Reporter: Roy Fulton

It was a misty night in the autumn of 1979 when Roy Fulton saw a figure signalling for a lift at the side of the road close to the village of Stanbridge in Bedfordshire. He was returning home from a darts match in a local pub, but has insisted that he had taken only a couple of drinks in the course of the evening. The hitchhiker was a pale young man, dressed only in a white shirt and dark trousers. Fulton pulled to a stop and asked him where he was going. The young man merely pointed in the direction of Dunstable, further along the road; because he said nothing, and looked disoriented, Fulton thought that he might be mute, or in some way mentally disturbed. However, Fulton indicated the back seat of his car and the man climbed in. For some minutes Fulton drove on, at about 65 km/h (40mph). Then: 'I turned round to offer him a cigarette – and the bloke had disappeared. I braked and had a quick look in the back to see if he was there. He wasn't, and I just gripped the wheel and drove like hell.'

Soon after, he reported the occurrence to the local police but, although they – and a reporter from the *Dunstable Gazette* who subsequently interviewed him – were impressed with his credibility, there seemed little that they could do. Nevertheless, Fulton remained convinced that he had given a lift to someone, and that this someone

Who is more scared: the driver or the hitchhiker? When Roy Fulton found that the man he'd given a lift to had disappeared, he was spooked. But perhaps the man had jumped out earlier because *he* was scared.

had vanished from the car without trace while it was moving at speed.

COMMENTARY:

This story has been chosen because, like the experiences reported above, it rests upon personal testimony. However, unlike the previous two reports, it is uncorroborated by any other witness. In addition, there is the distinct possibility that the young man accepted Fulton's lift, opened the rear door, then changed his mind and closed it again before climbing in – leaving Fulton with the impression that he had a passenger, which proved false when he subsequently looked around.

A TIMELY WARNING

Place: Palavas-les-Flots, near Montpellier, France

Time: 20 May 1981

Reporter: Hilary Evans

Late in the evening of 20 May 1981, two couples were returning to Montpellier after an outing to a nearby beach. The car was a two-door Renault 5, the two men seated in front and the two women behind. As they turned away from the sea at Palavas-les-Flots, a girl in white stood by the side of the road and, although the small car was full, the driver stopped because he thought it unsafe for a girl to be out alone at that time of night.

He announced that he was driving into Montpellier; the girl nodded, but did not speak. The other man then got out of the car, so that his seat could be folded forward, enabling the girl to squeeze in between the women in the back seat. As the driver continued on his way into Montpellier, the hitchhiker suddenly shouted: 'Look out for the turns! Look out for the turns! You're risking death!' As the driver slowed, the two women in the back seat screamed because, even as the hitchhiker cried out, she had vanished.

It was clearly impossible that she could have escaped from the car, but the shaken party stopped and searched the surroundings. Then, mystified, they reported the incident to an Inspector Lopez at Montpellier gendarmerie. As Lopez later stated: 'Their panic was not assumed, and we soon realized that they were genuine. It disturbed us.'

COMMENTARY:

In his book *Visions, Apparitions and Alien Visitors*, Hilary Evans described this case and a very similar one that had been reported in 1976. This was at Bagnères, a long way from Montpellier. As in the case described, the car was also a two-door model, a new one that two young men from the town were trying out.

Once again, the passenger had to move the front seat forward so that the hitchhiker, a girl, could get into the car. And, as before, she warned them that the bends ahead were dangerous, and that there had been a number of accidents. The driver slowed down, and both men reassured their passenger. A few minutes later one said, over his shoulder: 'You see, Madame, other people may kill themselves here, but we got by all right.' When there was no reply, both men glanced behind them – and found the back seat empty.

The source for this second story is suspect: it first appeared in the French magazine *Lumières dans la Nuit*; and it may well have given birth to a number of similar tales. Hilary Evans reported that extensive changes have been made to the roads in the area, to make them safer – and whether the phantom hitchhiker has subsequently been encountered again is not known.

APPENDIX 1

GHOSTS: THE PRIMITIVE VIEW

Will the dead return? From the earliest times this has been a question that people have asked themselves, and the answer – or answers – lies at the heart of some of our most primitive myths.

Animist beliefs, the forerunners of the more sophisticated religions, invested everything – tree or stone, mountain, river or lake – with its own resident spirit, a spirit that must be addressed, respected and propitiated. Gradually, a hierarchy of these spirits was conceived, the concept of superior gods emerged, and eventually came the idea of a single supreme god, to whom the others, in various degrees, remained subservient.

And where did humankind fit into this scheme? Humans, clearly, were possessed of their own spirits, and all ancient religious systems came to believe that, at death, this spirit was released from the body to mingle with all the other invisibles.

But early religions did not suggest that the human spirit was carried away from its natural surroundings to some distant heavenly residence. Some African traditional beliefs, for example, do not accept that a person dies naturally: he or she ceases to live within the body because in some way they have been 'interfered with', either by other humans, or perhaps by evil-intentioned spirits. Accordingly, the dead are not thought of as gone, but rather as continuing to take part, in spirit form, in the life of the community.

It cannot truly be said that the followers of these traditional African religions 'worship' their ancestor spirits; rather, they are concerned for their well-being, ask their advice, beg for favours – sometimes even argue with them. The ghosts of the dead are believed to be still present, often within a personal possession or in some favourite place that they frequented during life, where they can be invoked and consulted.

In China, the ghosts of Buddhist belief were regarded as malevolent spirits from the Underworld. In this reproduction of a Chinese woodcut, a 'mountain spectre' terrorizes a waking man.

HOSTILE SPIRITS

Not all primitive religions, however, regard ghosts as benevolent. Some tribes of the South American jungle, for instance, view all spirits as hostile; they are regarded as dangerous influences that must be appeased, as though the fact of death has automatically made the spirit vindictive. Spells will be cast after a family death, to drive the ghost away; or the body may be buried at a distance, so that the ghost will be unable to find a way to return.

A similar view of ghosts was also to be found in Japan, after Buddhism replaced the earlier, animistic, Shinto religion.

African Bushmen, too, fear their ghosts. They pile heavy stones over a corpse, and then raise a mound of earth, in an attempt to ensure that the deceased's spirit cannot escape to do them harm.

VAMPIRES

In Southeast Asia, ghosts are almost invariably malevolent. Usually invisible, they can sometimes take on a visible form, and are described as huge and terrifying in appearance. They are reputed to feed on dead bodies, but are also believed to attack living persons, like vampires, when they are especially hungry or evilly disposed, and young children are therefore particularly at risk. They are also said to be responsible for the outbreak of epidemics of disease.

The belief in cannibal ghosts may reflect an earlier practice that survived until recently in the highlands of New Guinea. There it was a pious duty for the relatives and friends of those who fell in warfare to consume the dead body in a funeral ritual. This was attributed both to the primitive belief that the bravery of the deceased could thereby be transmitted to the survivors, and to the need to please the spirits who were expected to give aid in battle.

As in other cultures, the recently dead were thought to be reluctant to depart from their earthly homes, where, as ghosts, they could continue to watch over the actions of their relatives, sometimes interfering in an unexpected way. Misfortune was often attributed to the attack of some kinsman who had died not long before. Ancestors, the more distant dead, were generally regarded as benevolent, but so remote that their influence was minimal. Nevertheless, at a festival celebrating the harvest, or when a pig was given and killed, its spirit was offered to the appropriate ancestor.

Although many Native Americans lived comfortably with their ghosts, among the Navajo they were always regarded as maleficent. Those who died very old or in early infancy had no ghosts, but death by any other cause inevitably bred evil spirits. They would return in many forms: as other humans or as animals, or sometimes only as the sound of whistling in the dark. They brought disease, or other forms of attack, and to see one was a sure omen of death.

VOODOO SPIRITS

West Africans carried off as slaves to Haiti took their beliefs with them, and their word *vodun*, which meant spirit, has survived as 'voodoo'. The invocation of voodoo in the successful revolution led by Toussaint l'Ouverture in Haiti in the 1790s, which resulted in the liberation of the slaves, has ensured its continuing survival. Children are still taught not to get their heads wet, especially with dew, because water attracts spirits, and the human spirit lives in the head. Night is the time for bogies, and the doors and windows must be shut tight to keep them out – but the *loup-garou*, which sucks children's blood, can get through the thatch. Then there is the *tonton macoute*, a bogeyman figure who will carry the children off if they are not good. He became a terrifying reality, not just to children, during François 'Papa Doc' Duvalier's regime (1957–71), when the name was given to the thugs who were employed to terrorize political rivals.

Kindly and helpful or malicious and evil-working, ghosts have survived in the more primitive beliefs of peoples throughout the world for hundreds of years.

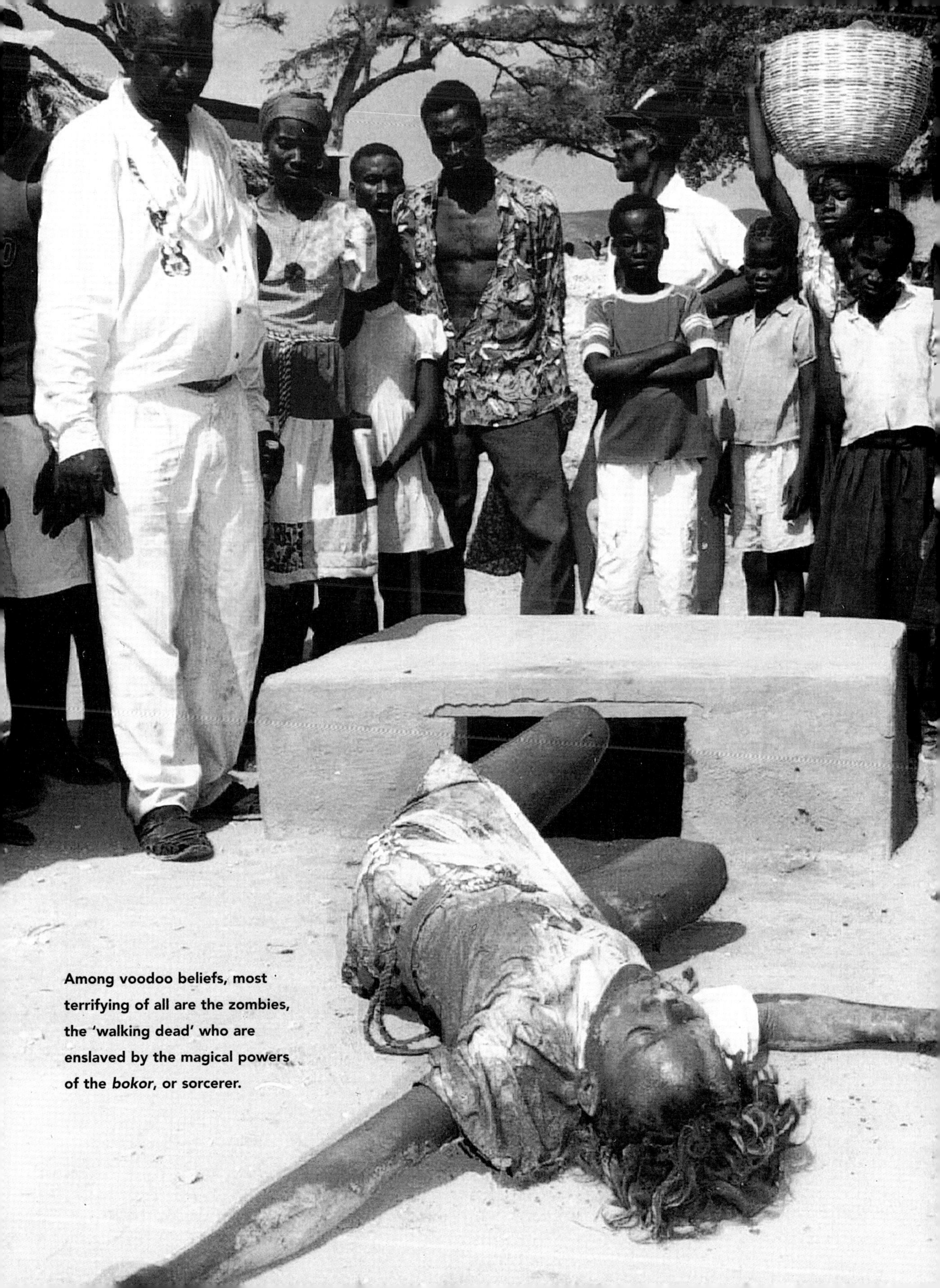

Among voodoo beliefs, most terrifying of all are the zombies, the 'walking dead' who are enslaved by the magical powers of the *bokor*, or sorcerer.

RAPHAEL
Rael

APPENDIX 2

SPIRITS AND THE SPIRIT WORLD

Necromancy, the ancient practice of communication with the dead, has been described as 'the blackest of all black arts'. In the 15th and 16th centuries it led to the disinterment of corpses and the rifling of graves, and the 1542 statute against witchcraft expressly condemned 'divers and sundry persons [who] unlawfully have devised and practised invocations and conjurations of spirits…' It is the more remarkable, therefore, that Spiritualism, which bases its beliefs upon the ability to communicate with those who have 'passed over', should be established as an acceptable religion, with its own churches and forms of worship.

The emotional force behind the development of modern Spiritualism was a backlash against the mechanistic view of the cosmos that, beginning with Descartes in the 17th century, had flowered during the 18th-century 'Age of Enlightenment'. The established churches were in disarray, unable to relate their dogma to discoveries concerning the structure and age of the universe, and the new theories of evolution. Ordinary people felt, like Hamlet, that 'there are more things in heaven and earth… than are dreamt of in your Philosophy'. Unable to obtain consolation from the Church, they turned instead to other beliefs that promised them the survival of the personality after death.

Necromancy was a forbidden practice for centuries. Many legends surround Dr John Dee, astrologer to Elizabeth I. Here he is seen, with his assistant Edward Kelly, summoning a corpse from the grave.

The modern Spiritualist movement traces its beginnings to the Fox sisters in Rochester, New York State, in 1849. Whether the phenomena that the sisters produced were fraudulent or not, they caused a quasi-scientific interest in 'mediumship' that swept the Western world. People who had attended a demonstration, or who had just heard about one, began to hold seances in their own homes, and soon societies of interested persons began to develop.

Spiritualism was introduced to Britain in 1852 by Mrs Maria B. Hayden, an American medium. In 1865, the Association of Progressive Spiritualists was the first to be formed, in Darlington, County Durham. Subsequent attempts to form a national organization were for a long time unsuccessful; eventually the Spiritualists' National Union Ltd was formed in 1902, and became the largest organization in Britain. Until the mid-20th century, Britain and the USA were the principal centres of Spiritualism. Recently the movement has grown rapidly in Latin America, particularly in Brazil, where it owes a great deal to African and American-Indian beliefs.

Although Spiritualism developed from a popular interest in psychical phenomena, it soon began to assume religious aspects. Many Spiritualists were in search of a system of belief to replace Christianity;

gradually, a ritual was instituted, avowedly to create a suitable atmosphere for communication with the spirit world, but closely resembling, in fact, that of the established churches, and by the 1870s many societies were describing themselves as 'churches'.

What do Spiritualists believe? Although it is difficult to generalize, there are certain beliefs that appear to be commonly held. Humankind, they say, is composed of two elements: a mortal body and an immortal spirit, or soul. At death, the spirit leaves the body, and enters a 'spiritual plane'. There are seven such planes, the earth being the lowest. The second plane, often referred to as 'Summerland', is a level of existence not unlike that on earth, except for the absence of any pain or suffering. And on this plane there is an opportunity for spiritual advancement comparable to that on earth.

Evil persons, after death, will find themselves alone in a kind of fog-bound limbo, and some Spiritualist societies have been known to organize 'rescue circles' designed to bring such lost souls to repentance. Those who have become too attached to material things find they are unable to leave the earthly plane, and these the Spiritualists believe appear as ghosts.

MESSAGES FROM THE SPIRIT WORLD

One of the most interesting experiments carried out in communication with the dead was devised by a group of members of the Society for Psychical Research. A number of friends agreed that, after their death, they would endeavour to send a series of messages to their friends still on earth. It is believed that, in order to make the experiment more convincing, they also agreed that each would send only a part of a message, so that the meaning of the whole would be apparent only when the various parts were compared. The participants included F. W. H. Myers, a noted classical scholar, and Edmund Gurney, both of whom had played an important part in the founding of the SPR; later came Henry Butcher, a professor of Greek, and Dr A. W. Verrall, another leading expert in the classics. The results that were obtained have been named 'cross correspondences'.

The full report on the experiment is complex, involving many obscure references to classical literature, and much ingenuity seems to have been employed in devising the messages. One early example must suffice.

On 16 April 1907, a Mrs Fleming, not a professional medium, who was in India, produced an automatic script that read 'Maurice. Morris. Mors. And with that the shadow of death fell upon him and his soul departed out of his limbs' – *mors* being Latin for 'death'.

The following day, in England, Mrs Leonora Piper, an American professional medium, the only one in the group, spoke the following words as she emerged from a trance: 'Sanatos… Tanatos' – and, a week later, '*thanatos*', the Greek for 'death'.

Another group member, Mrs Verrall, produced an automatic script on 29 April. It began with a slightly incorrect quotation from writer Walter Savage Landor – 'warmed both hands before the Fire of Life, it fails and I am ready to depart' – followed by the Greek letter delta, her symbol for death. Then she wrote a quotation in Latin from Virgil's *Aeneid* concerning the early death of the nephew of the emperor Augustus, and the first five words of a song in Shakespeare's *Twelfth Night*: 'Come away, come away, death'. Finally, she wrote out a long Latin quotation from the poet Horace concerning death.

In isolation, this example may not be particularly convincing: all the ladies were ready to receive messages from those they knew to be dead. In their entirety, however, the cross-correspondences are difficult to explain away. What is disappointing is that the participants in the experiments, if their spirits were genuinely engaged in these ingenious word games, were apparently unable to confirm or deny the fundamental tenets of Spiritualism.

What purported to be the spirit of Myers shall have the last word: 'The nearest simile I can find to express the difficulties of sending a message – is that I appear to be standing behind a sheet of frosted glass – which blurs sight and deadens sounds – dictating feebly – to a reluctant and somewhat obtuse secretary. A feeling of terrible impotence burdens me – I am powerless to tell what means so much – I cannot get into communication with those who would understand and believe me.' And so the experiment ended.

The development of photography during the 19th century coincided with the rise of Spiritualism. This 'psychic photograph' of a spirit appearing at a seance was allegedly obtained by Richard Boursnell in 1897.

APPENDIX 3

OUT-OF-BODY AND NEAR-DEATH EXPERIENCES

Researchers into the subject of apparitions of the living have inevitably compared the phenomena with 'astral projection' or out-of-body experiences. Very many people have, at one time or other, had such an experience: when the Institute of Psychophysical Research in Oxford carried out their first enquiry, they received details of more than 400 cases. These fall into two types, which have been named 'parasomatic' and 'asomatic'.

In a parasomatic type, the subject becomes aware of a duplicate body, a 'double': 'I looked down at my second self and found myself to be a complete replica of my material self. I touched my clothes, and looked at myself and was astounded to see that I was wearing the same black skirt, white blouse with small red spots on it, same shoes, etc… I can remember touching myself and feeling the texture of my clothing; this all felt quite solid…'

In an asomatic experience, the subject sees themself from another point of view without appearing to have any bodily form – just a disembodied state of consciousness, or, as one person put it, 'a pinpoint of presence'.

In many cases, the observing presence can see the 'double' continuing to function in an apparently normal way. A dentist, for example, described how he watched himself extract a tooth, while 'standing some three feet [one metre] behind myself and to the left'.

Experiences such as this seldom occur more than once or twice in a lifetime, but there are some people who claim to be able to leave their bodies at will. They have described various methods for attaining the desired state, all of which seem to have a common relationship. One involves a series of physical relaxation exercises; the second makes use of concentration and meditation; and the third requires the development of 'lucid dreams' – that is, a state in which the subject is aware that he or she is dreaming.

Practitioners of this 'astral projection' have made some startling claims. Commonest are cases in which the subject has 'floated' away from the body and visited another, unknown, location, that they

In his description of his experiences of 'astral projection', Sylvan J. Muldoon visualized his astral body as remaining attached to his physical body by a 'cord'.

were able to describe in detail, a description that they subsequently were able to confirm. This might be interpreted as telepathy, but other experiences are more puzzling. 'Astral travellers' have claimed to have visited the rooms of sleeping friends and disturbed objects on tables or shelves; there are even cases where the projected self has had conversations with others.

Although many out-of-body experiences take place, unexpectedly, during the course of everyday life, others occur when the subject is in a state of crisis, either emotional or physical. Whatever the case, the subject usually feels in a calm, joyful state, sometimes even excited and exhilarated: 'The escaped me felt absolutely wonderful,' said one person who had experienced it. 'Very light and full of the most wonderful vitality, in fact more well than I have ever felt before or since.'

And that brings us to what is called the 'near-death experience'. In recent years, the development of resuscitation techniques in operating theatres has resulted in patients being brought back, almost literally, 'from the brink of the grave'. For a brief period they have been clinically dead, but many have reported that, during this time, they have continued to have conscious experiences.

TOWARDS THE LIGHT

The first sensation is one of extreme calm, completely divorced from the frantic attempts at resuscitation taking place. This is generally succeeded by an out-of-body experience, in which the patient is aware of detachment from the body, and seems to be floating above it, able to observe themself and the activity taking place around them. Then comes the feeling of being propelled at speed along a dark tunnel towards a bright light. There is no sense of discomfort, and many people report a condition near ecstasy.

What next transpires has been claimed as firm evidence for the existence of life after death – and, by extension, a justification for the appearance of ghosts. The difficulty is that we must depend upon the patient's own interpretation of what is experienced, and it is clear that this is coloured by what they themselves expect to occur after death.

The experiences include: the appearance of a figure radiating love and compassion; a visit to

a beautiful garden or a 'city of light'; a review, described as being like a quick 'film show', of the subject's life; a vision of another reality in which 'all knowledge seems to co-exist beyond time and space'; and meetings with dead relatives and friends, who sometimes explain that the subject has arrived too soon, and must return to life on earth. This return is often described in terms of disappointment. Many people who have had a near-death experience choose to change their lives, particularly the spiritual dimension, because of it. But none of us will know, until the event, whether this is a true description of life after death.

In one of Sylvan J. Muldoon's 'astral projections', he was carried to a house where he saw a girl. Weeks later he encountered the girl and described her home in detail.

APPENDIX 4

AUTOMATIC ART FROM BEYOND THE GRAVE

Is Beethoven still at work on his *Tenth Symphony*? Does Albert Einstein have further contributions to make to our understanding of the cosmos? Is Picasso's brain still bubbling with images that must be transferred to paper?

These are questions that beg to be answered when we look at one of the most puzzling of psychical phenomena: the composition of works of art – drawings and paintings, musical scores, and a host of fictional, poetic and philosophic writings – by automatic means.

The term 'automatic' is used to describe the production of work that is not consciously directed by the person whose hand executes it. Psychologists make no sharp distinction between this activity and other 'dissociated' states: sleepwalking, loss of memory, habitual tics, multiple personality disorders, speaking in tongues, and the many manifestations of the trance condition. Those who produce the work, however, and all Spiritualists, have no doubt about the matter: they are in direct communication with the spirits of the dead artists whose compositions they reproduce.

Pearl Curran of St Louis, who for nearly 25 years was the spiritual vehicle for the writings of 'Patience Worth', which included poetry, plays and two novels.

Some automatists go into deep trance, and apparently have no consciousness of what they are doing; others are in near-trance, just somewhat drowsy; some are awake, but withdrawn into themselves; but others remain fully conscious, and can even carry on a conversation while their hands are at work. Awareness of the hands' movements can also vary greatly: some automatists know and can discuss what they are producing; some, while remaining conscious, have no idea what they are writing or drawing; some are unaware even that their hands are moving.

Leaving aside the written prophecies produced by seers throughout the centuries since the ancient Greek Oracle of Delphi, among the earliest examples of automatic writing are *Spirit Teachings* (1873) by W. Stainton Moses, often described as the 'bible' of British Spiritualism, and W. T. Stead's *After Death* (1897). Writings of this sort, however – famously described by the psychologist William James as 'in a curiously vague optimistic philosophy-and-water… as if one author composed more than half of the trance messages' – are very different from most later productions.

PATIENCE WORTH

The case of 'Patience Worth', for instance, has puzzled commentators for more than 80 years. It began in May 1913, in the city of St Louis, where Mrs Pearl Curran and some neighbours were lightheartedly consulting a Ouija board, and found it struggling to spell out 'Pat-C' over and over again. A month later it wrote: 'Oh why let sorrow steel thy heart? Thy bosom is but its foster-mother, the world its cradle and the loving home its grave' – an impressive but obscurely expressed sentiment. And then, on 8 July, the board announced that the communications came from 'Patience Worth'.

For nearly 25 years, Mrs Curran was the vehicle for Patience's writings, many of them of a marked literary quality, although her personal messages were in a strange archaic English that seemed an eclectic mixture of regional dialects. Patience did not give much detail about herself, claiming only to have been a Quaker girl born in Dorset in the 17th century, whose family had emigrated to America, where she had been killed by Indians shortly after.

As well as a good deal of poetry, Patience also dictated plays and two long novels. Her first, *The Sorry Tale* (1917), was composed every evening over a space of two years. It is set in Jerusalem at the time of Christ, and shows a detailed knowledge of Roman and Jewish customs, religious sects, contemporary politics and events, as well as domestic practices and the layout of the city itself.

The second novel, *Hope Trueblood* (1918), is an emotional story of the life of an illegitimate girl in Victorian England. It was published not only in America, but in England, where its unusual origins were unknown, and where it was well reviewed for its 'sheer excellence… [and its] sufficient high-grade characters, splendidly fashioned, to stock half a dozen novels'. Patience's third major work was *Telka: an Idyll of Medieval England* (1928), a 60,000-word epic poem.

Mrs Curran and her writings were investigated by Walter Franklin Prince of the Boston Society for Psychical Research, who was convinced that she had neither the vocabulary nor the knowledge necessary to produce these works herself, and that she could not subconsciously have reproduced them from memory of her very limited reading.

In terms of literary quality, these writings of 'Patience Worth' are the most outstanding examples of automatism; there have been others, notably by Geraldine Cummins (*When Nero was Dictator*, 1939), and by the Brazilian Francisco Candido Xavier.

As for musical compositions, the most prolific automatist has been a London housewife, Rosemary Brown, who produced original work in the style (and allegedly from the hand) of Liszt, Beethoven, Brahms, Debussy, Chopin, Schubert and Stravinsky. Professional musicians have declared themselves highly impressed with the pieces. In the course of being filmed by an American television company in October 1980, Mrs Brown scored a *Mazurka in D Flat*, which she claimed was communicated to her by Chopin.

AUTOMATIC ART

Automatic drawing and painting is in a rather different category when it comes to proposing a non-psychical explanation of the phenomenon. Nearly everyone is familiar with reproductions of the work of many different artists from many

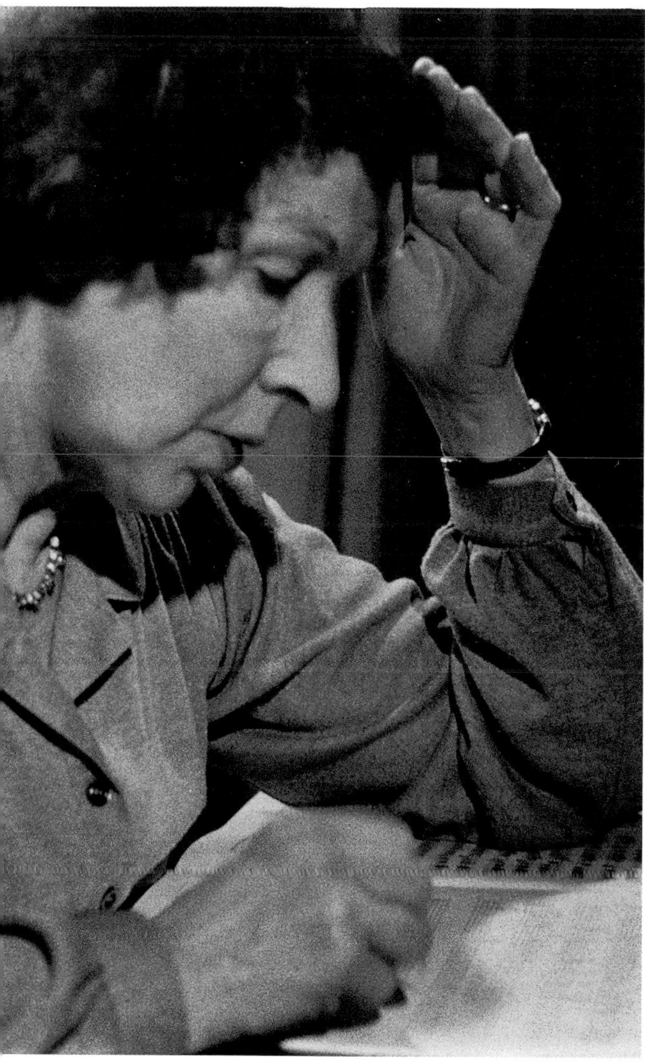

Rosemary Brown transcribing a *Mazurka* that she claimed had come from the spirit of Frédéric Chopin.

different periods; given sufficient graphic ability – an 'artist's eye' – we might think that we too could produce a fair copy of a well-known work. Art experts have often taken this line, too, explaining away automatic art as being merely the physical reproduction of a complete ('eidetic') image held in the subconscious memory.

Certainly this might be said of the work produced automatically by the English psychic Matthew Manning. His art includes an enormous diversity of drawings and paintings produced as a teenager in the 1970s: works signed Dürer, Beardsley, Klee, Picasso, da Vinci – even Beatrix Potter. Some, though notably close in style to the artist who is supposed to have inspired them, are original, but many are good – though not exact – copies of well-known masterpieces. Dürer's famous woodcut of a rhinoceros, for example, is drawn, and, although in the artist's detailed style, is obviously by a more amateurish hand. And – very oddly – a crayon clearly in the style of Raoul Dufy is signed 'Monet'.

Very different are the paintings of the Brazilian Luiz Gasparetto. Whereas Manning sat quietly, always aware of everything going on around him, until the page of his drawing pad was filled with what was obviously a carefully planned work of art, Gasparetto flings himself in a frenzy at the canvas, scooping up handfuls of paint and smearing them wildly about for a minute or two, until he achieves his purpose, signing the work, perhaps, 'Van Gogh' – something, in fact, that the artist never did, limiting himself to a simple 'Vincent'.

These are just a few of the 'stars' of automatic art, but the practice of producing writings and drawings that spring from the unconscious mind, whether or not in a state of trance, is widespread. Without claiming the inspiration of the famous dead, many mediums produce drawings said to be recognizable portraits of someone's departed relative, or written messages not in their own hand.

There is no suggestion that any of these automatic artists is fraudulent: whatever the standard of the work they produce – and it is often of a considerably higher quality than they are capable of in a fully conscious state – they themselves are convinced that they are in touch with the spirits of the dead.

APPENDIX 5

GHOSTS: TOWARDS AN EXPLANATION

What is a ghost? To many people, and certainly to all Spiritualists, the answer is a simple one: a ghost is the spirit of someone dead, which has either not yet 'passed over' to a higher plane of existence, or which revisits the scenes of its former life.

To the physical scientist, on the other hand, the question is unanswerable. It is a tenet of science that observations made and reported by one scientist can be replicated, given the skill and the equipment, by any other scientist. Ghosts cannot be reliably photographed, soun d recordings are at best dubious and cannot be properly analyzed, and no one has been able to persuade a ghost to appear at a specific time and produce detectable physical phenomena.

Given these problems, and the fact that an explanation for ghosts cannot be derived from any of the current theories of the nature of matter, most scientists react in a typical way: if something cannot be explained, it is much better to assume that it does not exist.

F. W. H. Myers, a well-known classical scholar and one of the founders of the Society for Psychical Research, was the author of *Human Personality and its Survival of Bodily Death* (1903). He also played a major role (after his death) in the 'cross-correpondences' experiment.

GHOSTS AND TELEPATHY

The Society for Psychical Research – which, over the years, has included in its membership a number of scientists who are prepared to keep an open mind on the matter – has tended to hold the middle ground. Their investigations of ghostly phenomena have gone hand in hand with their attempts to establish the existence of telepathic communication, and in the beginning they set out to discover whether 'hallucinations' were, in fact, images transmitted by telepathy between two 'sensitive' persons.

This, of course, begs the question as to whether telepathy genuinely occurs, and this is not the place to discuss the matter. However, many carefully controlled experiments, particularly in the Parapsychology Department of Edinburgh University, have lent substance to the belief that some kind of non-physical communication can take place between the mind of one person and that of another.

This raises a very interesting problem, and one that the SPR was faced with as soon as the results of its 1894 Census of Hallucinations were analyzed. Many of the experiences reported were images of people who were dead, and who appeared to be trying to establish communication with the living. It is all very well to hypothesize that some hitherto-

The aeronautical engineer J. W. Dunne developed a fascinating theory of the nature of time, which may help to explain the phenomenon of ghosts.

undetectable form of communication can occur between the minds of living persons, but how can the dead make use of the same faculty?

This question was addressed by one of the founders of the SPR, F. W. H. Myers, in his *Human Personality and its Survival of Bodily Death* (1903), and later by G. N. M. Tyrrell in *The Personality of Man* (1947). We are all conscious that we exist, conscious in a way that we suppose other living organisms, plants and most animals, are not. This sense of 'being' seems to be independent of the body, or of the normal operations of the brain, and has given rise to the concept of the soul. Call it what you will – soul, spirit, personality – this separate entity, it is suggested, survives death and can communicate in the same transcendental way as it could have done during life.

But how and where does this entity survive? Carl Jung, who, following a number of personal experiences, firmly believed in ghosts, telepathy, and other psychical phenomena, proposed the existence of a 'collective unconsciousness' in which we all share, and in which the sum 'memory' of all human existence is stored.

This, however, does not explain why some apparitions occur only at the moment of death or shortly after, while many seem gradually to fade with time. Another theory presupposes the existence of some kind of field of force, comparable in a way to the electrostatic or magnetic field, or perhaps even more so to the wave-mechanical picture of atomic structure. Everything, both physical and mental, is represented by concentrations of energy at points within this field. At death, the physical energy is rapidly dissipated, but the mind's energy can remain concentrated for a considerable time. Those who are telepathic in life, or who establish communication with the dead, are able to 'tune in' to specific areas of the force field, rather as a radio can be tuned to receive a single broadcast signal out of the vast range of signals that pass through the atmosphere every second.

A simple analogy may help to visualize how ghostly entities survive in this force field. Anyone who has rowed a boat gently across a lake on a calm evening knows that, as the oars lift from the water, they create intense little eddies, which spiral away through the water. These eddies can be seen moving away over the lake, gradually giving up their energy, but still evidence that a boat has passed. In the same way, we may suppose that an intense experience – pain, shock or whatever – can cause a vortex in the force field that, after death, will maintain its energy and be capable of detection. The possibility of this hypothetical force field can also explain poltergeist phenomena – rather more than any other theory can.

PARALLEL UNIVERSES

Yet another theory for ghosts relies upon the nature of time. Most scientists insist that time moves only forward – they speak of the 'arrow of time' – and, just as we cannot move backward in time, so we cannot look forward. Einstein, however, in formulating his concept of the space-time continuum, pointed out that the three spatial dimensions and the single time dimension cannot be distinguished from one another: all everyday experience is within a four-dimensional frame. From this it can be argued that, just as spatial dimensions exist whatever the time, so all time – past, present and future – can co-exist in an infinity of parallel universes.

This theory was developed by the mathematician and engineer J. W. Dunne. Although Dunne did not specifically consider the phenomenon of ghosts, it is tempting to propose that, when someone 'sees' a ghost, they are somehow looking out from their own timeframe and observing events in another.

The psychical researcher G. N. M. Tyrrell. He joined the Society for Psychical Research in 1908 and, after an early career in the development of radio, devoted his life to the study of psychical phenomena.

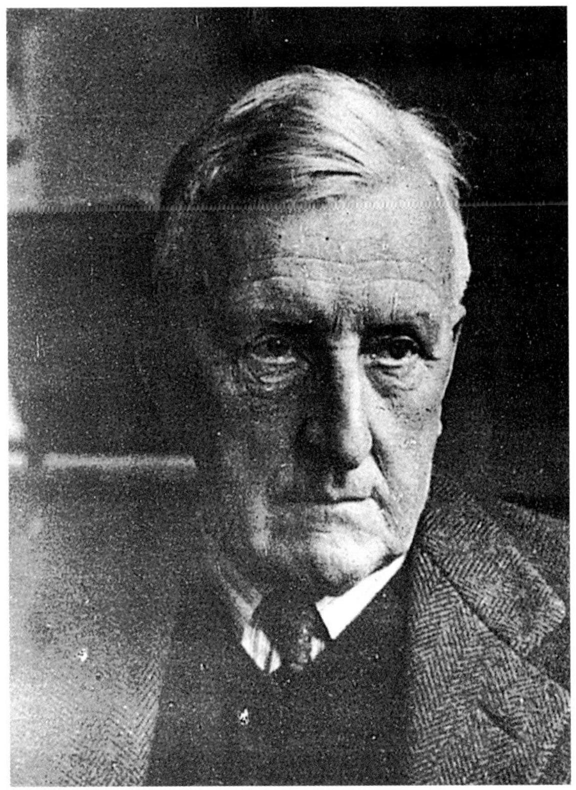

APPENDIX 6

GHOSTS IN FICTION

There are many ghosts in classical literature, and in the epic literature of the Dark Ages, but these can scarcely be counted as fiction: those who composed tales about them generally – and their audiences certainly – believed in their historical reality. In fact, before the emergence of prose fiction in the 17th century, the only notable appearances of non-historic ghosts were on the stage.

If we allow the necromantically-raised spirit of Helen in Marlowe's *Dr Faustus* (1594) to be considered a ghost, this is probably the first major work to include one – but with reservations: since Faustus was a real person, Marlowe may well have believed in the actuality of his pact with Mephistopheles. Even Shakespeare's most renowned ghosts – those of Hamlet's father, and of Banquo in *Macbeth* – appear in what he regarded as dramatic interpretations of history.

Truly fictional ghosts make their appearance with the vogue for the mid-18th-century 'Gothic' novels, such as *The Castle of Otranto* (1765), of which its author, Horace Walpole, wrote: 'I gave rein to my imagination, visions and passions choked me.' These Gothic stories were usually set among haunted castles, graveyards, and other picturesque and evocative sites. Later celebrated practitioners of the genre include Mary Shelley, Edgar Allan Poe and Sheridan Le Fanu, but their tales tended more to horror than to the purely supernatural.

The ghost of Jacob Marley appearing to Ebenezer Scrooge in what may be the first fully developed ghost story – Charles Dickens's *A Christmas Carol*.

Washington Irving gathered and embroidered the folktales of the old Dutch settlers in America in the early 19th century, such as in *The Legend of Sleepy Hollow*, but what may be the first example of a fully developed 'ghost story' is Charles Dickens's *A Christmas Carol* (1843). This features no fewer than four ghosts – that of Jacob Marley, and the spirits of Christmas Past, Christmas Present, and Christmas Yet to Come – and includes the clanking chains, and portentous knockings and footsteps, that played so dramatic a part in Pliny's tale of Athenodorus's ghost, and were an essential ingredient of many tales by lesser writers. Ghosts also appear in several of Dickens's short stories. Eight years after *A Christmas Carol*, Charlotte Brontë's novel *Villette* includes the ghost of a nun, 'buried here alive… beneath the ground which now bears us.'

From this time forward, more and more authors began to turn their hand to the subject of ghosts. Throughout the 19th century, the Western world was drawn to psychical matters, and fiction writers were only too willing to feed this interest. Wilkie Collins was a close friend and collaborator of

Playful ghosts: Rex Harrison is haunted by Kay Hammond's ghost in Noël Coward's *Blithe Spirit.*

horror, as in the writings of H. P. Lovecraft; or they became increasingly flippant.

But Susan Hill's short novel *The Woman In Black* (1983), which became a long-running stage play, also shows that there is still interest in an old-fashioned ghost story. And Stephen King's novel *The Shining* (1977), in which a boy's psychic powers allow him to 'see' the horrific past of the hotel where his family is snowbound, follows in the Lovecraftian tradition.

More recently, Lindsay Clarke's novel *The Chymical Wedding* (1989) and A. S. Byatt's novel *Possession* (1990) have added new dimensions to the ghost story.

Dickens, and in novels such as *The Haunted Hotel* (1879) he maintained the tradition.

By the end of the century, the ghost story had become an established literary form, one that leading authors were happy to experiment with, as in Oscar Wilde's *The Canterville Ghost* (1887). Henry James set the seal on the style with his masterly *The Turn of the Screw* (1898), which he described as 'a trap for the unwary'. This tale of the ghosts of the evil ex-valet Peter Quint and his mistress, the former governess Miss Jessel, and their guilty involvement with two children, builds literary horror upon horror.

The finest collections of macabre short stories are *Ghost Stories of an Antiquary* (1904) by the biblical scholar M. R. James. His closest rival – although not in the same class – is Algernon Blackwood, whose collection *The Empty House*, published in 1906, was followed by more than 30 books.

With the increased scepticism of the 20th century, ghost stories took two separate directions: they either advanced deeper into the realms of

Romantic ghosts: Rex Harrison – a ghost this time – haunts the new home of Gene Tierney in *The Ghost and Mrs Muir.*

Comedy ghosts: Michael Keaton plays a zany ghost in the madcap comedy *Beetlejuice*.

GHOSTS ON SCREEN

The medium of cinema has for a century now offered the opportunity to depict convincing ghosts. Admittedly, the treatment has often been quite lighthearted, from Noël Coward's play and film *Blithe Spirit*, to friendly ghosts, such as *Casper*, malicious comedy ghosts, such as those fought in the *Ghostbusters* films, and romantic ghosts reconnecting with their living partners, as in *Ghost* (1990).

But horror films still use ghosts to spook their audiences, such as Stanley Kubrick's film of Stephen King's *The Shining* (1980) or *Poltergeist* (1982), which made spectacular use of advances in special effects' technology, the *Insidious* series (2011–) and the *Paranormal Activity* films (2007–), where the story is told through the supposed found footage of security cameras and camcorders. The fake found footage wave was itself launched with *The Blair Witch Project* (1999), in which three student filmmakers disappear into the woods in Maryland while shooting a documentary about a local legend of a haunting.

In recent years, East Asian cinema has also proved very successful at making disturbing ghostly horror films, namely *Ringu* (1998) from Japan, and the Singapore–Hong Kong film *The Eye* (2002), both of which were remade in Hollywood.

More psychologically, classically Gothic ghost stories on screen include *The Innocents* (1961), a version of James's *The Turn of the Screw*, *The Others* (2001), which shares many similarities with *The Innocents*, and *The Sixth Sense* (1999), where a child psychologist meets a troubled boy who can communicate with ghosts.

Given that we believe in ghosts no less than we did a hundred years ago, it seems likely that writers and filmmakers will continue to tell ghost stories in fiction, whether they are comic or romantic, soothing, unsettling or shocking.

In *Ghost*, Patrick Swayze's spirit returns to his grief-stricken widow, played by Demi Moore.

INDEX

PICTURE CREDITS

Ace Photo Agency: 186
Alamy: 6 (Painting), 34/35 (Washington Imaging), 56 (Chronicle), 76 (A. F. Archive), 77 (David Grossman), 86/87 (Fuller Photography), 104/105 (Greg Balfour Evans), 120 (A. F. Archive), 123 (A. F. Archive), 146/147 (Tristar Photos), 160 (HIP), 182 (Keith Beaty/Toronto Star), 196 (Insomnia)
Bridgeman Art Library: 84
Corbis: 12 (Gerard Labriet/Photononstop), 54/55 (Adam Woolfitt), 101, 102/103
Courtauld Insititute: 54
Depositphotos: 29 (Bennymarty), 47 (Nicolaivanovici), 52/53 (Pitamaha), 116/117 (Acceloratorhams), 159 (Vicspacewalker)
Dreamstime: 70/71 (Christine48ers)
Fortean Picture Library: 8, 9, 21, 32, 37, 65, 66/67, 96, 108, 126/127, 131, 141, 142/143, 144, 152/153, 158, 161, 177, 194, 195 both, 202, 208/209, 214, 216, 217, 218
Getty Images: 27(Apic), 28 (Pat English), 38/39, 58/59, 72 (Popperfoto), 88/89 (Hulton), 91 (Popperfoto), 99, 138/139 (Brian Brainerd), 167–169 (Nina Leen), 173 (Ullstein Bild), 188, 192 (Quavondo), 205 (Popperfoto)
Images Colour Library/Charles Walker Collection: 14, 19, 20, 50/51, 57, 137, 156, 206
Kobal Collection: 119
Mary Evans Picture Library: 7, 10, 11, 17, 18, 22, 24, 37, 60, 63, 68 (Harry Price), 78, 80, 81, 111, 128, 130, 148, 163, 164/165, 166, 176, 178/179, 180, 210, 213
Page One Photography: 75
Public Domain: 16
Ronald Grant Archive: 150/151, 220-221 all
Simon Marsden: 30, 42, 48, 62, 92/93, 94, 95, 106, 124, 134/135, 140
Smithsonian Institution: 83
Syndication International: 44/45
The Sun: 26
TopFoto: 171, 184/185 (AP)